T0208207

A **Revelation** of
Life Endeavors

A **Revelation** of
Life Endeavors

Gangs for Jesus

THOMAS REMBERT JR

A REVELATION OF LIFE ENDEAVORS
GANGS FOR JESUS

iUniverse books may be ordered through booksellers or by contacting:

iUniverse
1663 Liberty Drive
Bloomington, IN 47403
www.iuniverse.com
1-800-Authors (1-800-288-4677)

ISBN: 978-1-5320-9285-5 (sc)
ISBN: 978-1-5320-9286-2 (e)

Print information available on the last page.

iUniverse rev. date: 01/09/2020

To South Carolina State University, the United States Army, and the New York City Housing Authority, all three of these resources taught me to be responsible and accountable to all of the decisions you make in life, both pros and cons, because the blame is on you, as you will "reap what you sow."

To my family—my wife, children, and grandchildren—who taught me that love is unconditional.

Contents

Preface

Empathy, sympathy, and compassion for others is truly missing in much of our society, especially in many of the top positions in the world. Why can't we realize that it is not about ourselves but our care for others? Building walls to separate people or building bridges to unite them is a major concern as we struggle with immigration, division, separation of children from their parents, and a drug epidemic eating at the core of our existence.

What should we do? Should we be arrogant and conceited and win at all costs, or should we show love, respect, and compassion for all races? Should we allow open borders to all nations, provided they are willing to work, pay taxes, and provide self-sufficiency for their families? Should we deny entrance to our country for certain races, or should we realize that our families were once immigrants who came to this country to get away from tyrannical governments or just find a better way of life? Are we willing to lie to cover up a bad past that is bound to negatively affect our present or future, or are we willing to lie, cheat, or steal to get rich? What should we do about homosexuals, lesbians, and same-sex marriages? Should they have the same rights as the divine principles of marriage between a man and woman? What are your views on many of these issues as they are all about life endeavors?

Introduction

Will there ever be peace in our lifetime? Perhaps never. If you are rich, you don't ever want to think about being poor. And if you are poor, you want to be rich but have long since accepted the fact that it is unlikely that you will become rich. Peace will come when all people make a concerted effort to rid the world of poverty and hunger through a serious sharing of their wealth.

God created all of us in His image, but humankind absolutely refuses to accept this divine principle of life. We are still trying to find DNA that makes us different instead of searching for things in life that make us the same. When we accept the fact that all people are created equal in God's image, peace will come, but this may never happen.

A Revelation of Life Endeavors was created to rid the world of the outside forces that make us different, for instance, money, pride, greed, poverty, crime, drugs, racism, education, religion, lying, cheating, stealing, and all the other atrocities in the world that zap our spiritual qualities that were instilled in humankind when God said, "Let us make man in our image, after our likeness, so God created man in his own image in the image of God created He, male and female." (Genesis 2:27 KJV).

A Revelation of Life Endeavors is about bringing people of all races back to God instead of humankind with Satan's influences and the trappings of the world affecting people's thought process and causing them to hear, "If you want to get rich, it is okay to lie, cheat, or steal" instead of saying that it is flat-out wrong.

A Revelation of Life Endeavors is a fascinating journey into the world of the downtrodden families whose lives are etched in poverty and despair, always searching for a way to improve their plight. Through a series of instructional lectures and essays on how to deal with the myriad of problems facing us in society—immigration, welfare, poverty, racism, drugs, and weapons of mass destruction—I paint a picture of the downtrodden rising out of the ashes of despair and achieving the epitome of success. I do this through a series of essays on secular and religious subjects designed to motivate and improve the plight of each of us through education, self-improvement, and a close affiliation with God and His Son, Jesus, as the foundation of our lives.

I have seen firsthand what love, hatred, and the absence of strong father figures can do to an ordinary family, causing them to become wards of society who have succumbed to drugs and prostitution. Come with me as I wave my magic wand to eliminate the many perils that confront us in society as we deal with children using drugs and weapons of mass destruction. The lectures are truly inspirational, motivational, and thought-provoking, as I deal with emotions of love, peace, and hatred that are destroying our society.

In summary, *A Revelation of Life Endeavors* is about secular matters as they relate to humankind's destruction because secular matters are based on worldly events, for example, money, pride, and greed controlled by humankind but influenced by the devil.

I realized at a young age that people will fail you. They will lie, cheat, or steal to advance their cause and take you only so far, but God will take you across the finish line. As I reflect on my childhood, I always believed that there was a power greater than humankind, and I became fascinated by the Bible because it taught me to see that power. I became humbled.

I am just a nobody trying to tell somebody about God and His Son, Jesus Christ. God has always provided for me. I have never lost a fight because I fought out of fear and with God's protection. I was an enforcer at the age of six as well as a master mediator because I was the smartest and strongest in my age group as well as beyond. God gave me almost photographic memory, as I could memorize full chapters of biblical scriptures and recite them on Easter Sunday during the Easter programs that we had at our church. I came out of high school on an accelerated program with God's divine hands always by my side as I began my climb to the top.

To deal with the myriad of secular issues in our lives, I realized that only a spiritual revolution to bring us back to God could solve these issues. On March 5, 2007, I started an organization called Gangs for Jesus to help address the spiritual and religious aspects of our lives. At present, there are sixteen essays of religious subjects based on the teachings of Jesus Christ, as is portrayed in the Sermon on the Mount or the Beatitudes, as it is commonly called. (See Matthew 5–7 KJV).

1. Life, Liberty, and the Pursuit of Happiness
2. The Modification of Christianity
3. The Entrance of Sin into the World
4. What Are God's Plans for Humankind?
5. What Must I Do to Be Saved?
6. God Has the Power to Do What Humans Cannot Do
7. Repent and Live or Stay Wicked and Die
8. Qualities of People Chosen by God
9. God Resists the Proud but Gives Grace to the Humble
10. Why Is the World in Such a Mess?
11. God's Plan for Humankind Is to Prosper, Provided They Are in the Delight of the Lord
12. The Spirit of God
13. God Is
14. Healing the World
15. The Riches of the Righteous
16. Ask for the Right Thing

As I reflect today, more than twelve years since the formation of Gangs for Jesus, my goal is still the same: to teach the world how to live in peace and prosperity for all races of people.

Who am I? I am a teacher and a preacher seeking to recruit disciples for Jesus who are so fervent about Jesus that they are like gang members, totally committed to the call of the righteous. I am a teacher and a preacher for the peace and prosperity of all of humankind, not just for the 10 percent of the population who owns 90 percent of the wealth in the world.

This is *A Revelation of Life Endeavors*.

Ask for the Right Thing

B e careful what you ask for. It may not be the right thing. Most people would ask for money if they had a chance to receive anything they asked for. What would you ask for if you could receive anything you asked for? Would it be money? I hope not, for money is the way of the world.

Let's look at a few important personalities in the Bible, Solomon and Elisha. David gave orders to his son, Solomon, to be strong and "show thyself a man and keep the orders of the Lord, your God to walk in his ways, to keep his statues, his commandments, and his testimonies, as it written in the law of Moses so you may prosper in all that you do and wherever you turn yourself." (1 Kings 2: 3 KJV)

Solomon had been given his orders but knew he needed God's help to carry them out. He did not need money in order to become this person whom he had been charged to become. He needed God. The story goes on to say that the Lord appeared to Solomon while in Gibeon in a dream by night. God said, "Ask what I shall give you."

Solomon said to God, "Give your servant an understanding heart to judge your people." For a Biblical reference see 1 Kings 3: 8-9 KJV.

God was pleased with Solomon's request and gave him a wise and understanding heart so that there was none like him before and none after him. Because Solomon was humble and obedient and this pleased God, he was also given abundant riches and honor like no other king before or after him.

The moral of the story is that Solomon asked for an understanding heart, not money, which so pleased God that He rewarded him with abundant riches as well. For a biblical reference, look at 1 Kings 1–4 and 11 KJV.

Solomon did his best to walk in the Lord's ways, but he failed because he had a weakness for many strange women. In fact, the Bible states he had seven hundred wives and princesses as well as three hundred concubines. His wives turned away his heart, and his heart was not perfect with God, as it was with the heart of David, his father. God was very displeased because Solomon had done evil in His sight because he had turned to the gods of his wives and violated God. For it is written "No man can serve two masters: for either he will hate the one and love the other; or else he will hold to the one and despise the other. Ye cannot serve God and mammon." (Matthew 6:24 KJV)

Solomon disobeyed the very first commandments of God by following after other gods that his many wives had convinced him to follow. God is the one and only true God. The key thing to remember, however, is that Solomon asked God for an understanding heart to be able to judge his people but failed to keep all of God's commandments because he had a weakness for women. Solomon had indeed asked God for the right thing, an understanding heart, and was greatly rewarded with an understanding heart and great riches as well. Ask for the right thing. Solomon did and was greatly rewarded.

Now let us look at Elisha. For a Bible reference, read 2 Kings 2:9 KJV, which states, "And it came to pass when they were gone over Elijah said to Elisha, 'Ask what I shall do for you before I am taken away from you.' And Elisha said, 'I pray thee, let a double portion of thy spirit be upon me."

Elisha had asked for a double portion of Elijah's spirit to fall upon him, and when Elijah was taken up, he was rewarded with it. What is the spirit of Elijah that fell upon Elisha?

We must look at this from a historical perspective. Elijah was a prophet during the time of King Arab and his wife, Jezebel. The Jews had already crossed over the Jordan River and begun the conquest of the Canaanites, the Hittites, Amorites, and the remainders of the land of the seven nations that God had promised to provide for them.

God had promised to provide them with a land flowing with milk and honey, but seven strong and powerful nations, which they feared the land, occupied the land. And due to a lack of real belief, they were never able to fully drive out these seven nations, even until today. That land would be the land of the present-day Middle East, beginning with the Persian Gulf, the Tigris and Euphrates Rivers, south to Egypt and the Nile River, west to the Mediterranean Sea, and north to the Lebanon Mountains to include Iraq and the surrounding areas of the Middle East.

They were able to reestablish present-day Israel, but God would never let them fully occupy all of this land, and they began to mingle with pagan gods. As a result, they were constantly punished and enslaved, but God always allowed a remnant to remain to honor His covenant and promise that He had made with Abraham, Isaac, and Jacob.

The Jews never did learn what to ask God for. Instead they looked to humankind and asked God to provide them with a king to deliver their enemies to them without believing that God had already given their enemies to them in His promise. By the time Elijah lived, idol worship of all types were in place, and God chose Elijah to prove that these gods and pagan religions under Baal, the god of the Canaanites who was supposed to have power over rain and the weather in general, had no concrete power in comparison with God's power.

Ahab was an evil king of Israel who was made worse by his marriage to Jezebel, a staunch believer of Baal. The two of them became staunch adversaries of Elijah because Elijah was able to defeat all of the pagan gods of King Ahab and his evil wife, Jezebel. In fact, Elijah prayed to God and caused a fire to rain down from heaven, which killed one hundred of Jezebel's soldiers, whom she had sent to capture Elijah after he had embarrassed her by defeating her gods made from wood, gold, silver, and so on.

Elijah was so powerful that he was able to raise the dead and cause it to rain, breaking a famine on the land that had lasted for three years. God had given Elijah the power to cause a drought and then bring rain

3

after it had not rained for more than three years. God allowed Elijah to be fed by a raven to avoid being captured by King Ahab and his wife, Jezebel. Elijah was so much a man of God that God allowed his prayers to be answered immediately in the presence of his enemies.

The spirit of Elijah is the spirit of belief. Elijah believed whatever you ask in prayer while believing you shall receive, and God proved it over and over. Elijah was not allowed to taste death but ascended into heaven by a whirlwind to be with God, so there is no wonder why His servant Elisha wanted a double portion of Elijah's spirit to fall upon him before his ascension into heaven. The spirit of Elijah is a spirit of faith and belief, a belief that no matter what the circumstances, God will provide a solution. Under all circumstances, trust God to deliver.

When we look at Elisha and Elijah, we learn to ask for the spirit of Elijah to fall upon us, which is the spirit of prayer and the belief that God will answer prayer no matter what the circumstances are. The second thing taken from Solomon is to ask God to provide us with an understanding heart to deal with our fellow humans in a righteous and just manner. The third thing is to ask God to provide us with the spirit of Jesus, which is the spirit of love and forgiveness.

The spirit of Jesus is based on the two principles of love and forgiveness. John 3:16 KJV states, "God so loved the world that he sent his only Begotten Son that whosoever believe in him shall not perish but have everlasting live." Matthew 18:21–22 KJV reads, "Then came Peter to him and asked the Lord how often shall by brother sin against me and I forgive him, should seven times be enough? Jesus answered not just seven times but until seventy times seven, which is four hundred and ninety times."

Based on this analogy, we should constantly be willing to forgive others for the wrong that is done to us. Jesus was so willing to forgive that even when He was being crucified, He said, "Lord forgive them for they know not what they are doing." (Luke 22: 34 KJV)

The key to knowing what to ask God for and when to ask for it is based on many principles, but we must keep in mind the following:

- Ask God for an understanding heart, as Solomon espoused, for proper treatment of your fellow human beings.
- Ask God for deliverance of all things through constant prayer with a belief that God will answer and it shall be received, as was done with Elijah.
- Ask God to allow you to love Him with all your heart, mind, body, and soul; to love your neighbor as yourself; and to be willing to forgive those who sin against you not just seven times but until seventy times seven.

Gangs for Jesus

G angs for Jesus was created on March 5, 2007. It is an organization designed to change the thinking of gangs or people in general from a radical and violent approach to life to one of peace and love through a close affiliation with Jesus Christ as the focal point in the fabric of their thinking. It is centered on three basic themes:

1. Learn to be humble.
2. Don't worship money and glamour.
3. Change from your current way of thinking.

One of the very first lessons taught by Jesus as He began His ministry was the message of humbleness. It is a message of meekness, humility, and a lack of extreme pride. This was first expressed when Jesus allowed John the Baptist to baptize Him, although both He and John the Baptist knew He was the Son of God. Matthew 3 depicts this story. Verses 13–17 KJV state,

> Then came to Jesus from Galilee to Jordan unto John to be baptized of him but John forbade Him saying I have need to be baptized of you and here you come to me. Jesus answered Him and said it is permitted to be so for us to fulfill all righteousness. And immediately upon His baptism the heavens were opened up and the

Spirit of God like a dove descended upon Jesus and then a voice from heaven said this is My Beloved Son, in whom I am well pleased.

Psalm 9:9-10 KJV states,

> The Lord will be a refuge for the oppressed, a refuge in the time of trouble and they that know the Lord will put their trust in Him and the Lord will not forsake them that seek Him. When He makes inquisition for the blood of man he remembers are oppressed and He does not forget the cry of the humble.

The Bible further states that God resists the proud but gives grace to the humble. There is no wonder why the very first message of Jesus's Sermon on the Mount states, "Blessed are the poor in spirit [the humble] for theirs is the kingdom of heaven." This quote comes from Matthew 5: 3 KJV.

The second basic theme for Gangs for Jesus is based on the principle of money, affluence, wealth, or however else you might describe the necessity for trying to get money. Jesus first expressed this aspect of greed in Matthew 4:1 KJV.

> Then was Jesus lead of the spirit into the wilderness to be tempted by the devil and when He had fasted forty days and forty nights he was afterward very hungry and the devil came to him knowing that He was hungry and said to Him, if you be the Son of God, command that these stones be made bread, and Jesus answered and said, "It is written man shall not live by bread alone, but by every word that proceeds out of the mouth of God."

Verse 8 states again the devil took Jesus up onto an exceedingly high mountain and showed Him all the kingdoms of the world and the glory of them. Jesus said to him,

Get away from me Satan for it is written you shall worship the Lord your God and only Him shall you serve. Although Jesus had the power to do whatever He wanted, He chose not to do so because He knew that the devil represented the kingdom of the world which is man's kingdom and not the word of God which is the kingdom of God.

Jesus did not allow Himself to be corrupted by the riches and the glory of the world because, what good is there to gain the whole world and lose your own soul? God promises us, however, that if we first seek the kingdom of God, all things will be added unto us. Money, power, and affluence will follow us when we give our lives to Jesus and follow His direction. There will be no need to worship money and commit all kinds of atrocities to gain money when the best path is to follow Jesus's teachings.

The third theme for the organization is repentance. This theme requires a change in mind-set. The requirement is that you must change from your old way of thinking and acting and substitute a new way of thinking, a fresh attitude. Jesus taught this best in His Sermon on the Mount, or the Beatitudes. It states,

1. Blessed are the poor in spirit, for theirs is the kingdom of heaven.
2. Blessed are those who mourn, for they shall be comforted.
3. Blessed are the meek, for they will inherit the earth.
4. Blessed are those who hunger and thirst for righteousness, for they will be filled.
5. Blessed are the merciful, for they will be shown mercy.
6. Blessed are the pure in heart, for they will see God.
7. Blessed are the peacemakers, for they will be called Sons of God.
8. Blessed are those who are persecuted because of righteousness, for theirs is the kingdom of heaven.
9. Blessed are you when people insult you, persecute you, and falsely say all kinds of evil against you because of Me. Rejoice

and be glad because great is your rewards in heaven, for in the same way, they persecuted the prophets who were before you.

The Beatitudes, as Jesus taught, are an excellent way to pattern our lives and a perfect scenario for changing our mind-sets and substituting a new pattern of thinking, belief, and action. The goal for Gangs for Jesus is based on this concept of humbleness, avoiding love for money and substituting a new pattern of thinking, actions, and beliefs. It is our belief that young people of all ages will benefit from this spiritual revolution, and it is our goal that the whole fabric of our thinking will revert to Jesus's teachings before and after He ascended into heaven.

God Is

"**M**y thoughts are not your thoughts, neither are your ways my ways," said the Lord (Isaiah 55:8 KJV). Who is God, or what is God? Is He the God of the Bible, or is He the God of humankind? Is He a *He* or not, or is God an *It* or not? Is the Bible the Word of God or the word of humankind? You need to know this to accept God's infallibility.

God is a Spirit, so He is neither man nor woman. God is God without any reservations, period. God is the universal creator of everything. Everything moves by God's power. Nothing exists unless God permits it. People have no control unless God allows it to be so. God is the Alpha and Omega, the Beginning and the End. You must accept that everything begins with God. He is the originator, the creative force that is able to create anything that He chooses.

Once we accept this as an undeniable fact, we can go with the universe as it exists and has always existed since the beginning of time. God is the beginning of time. There can never be peace until the world accepts this simple fact. We must also accept the fact that the Bible is the absolute word and power of God. When God speaks, everything changes just on the basis of His words. In essence, He speaks it into existence.

God has unlimited power. He can do what humankind cannot do. He makes the clouds appear, the rain fall, and the sun shine. God's power moves everything. Nothing exists without His ability to create or destroy matter. Science will say that matter cannot be created or destroyed, but God can create or destroy matter.

The Bible is the story of God's love for humankind. We were made in God's image to give Him pleasure. Our first purpose in life is to give God pleasure by living a righteous life, and God will provide us with our hearts' desires. God knows the way of the righteous, but the way of the ungodly shall perish (see Psalm 1:6). He shall be like a tree planted by the rivers of waters that brings forth His fruit in His season. His leaf shall not wither, and whatsoever He does shall prosper (see Psalm 1:3).

You see, God intended for us to prosper, provided we remain righteous toward Him to receive His blessings, the blessings of Abraham. God promised to provide for us because of His love for us. He loved us so much that He sent His only begotten Son so we would have the right to the tree of life. But by the time Jesus came, humans had become so distant from God that it was impossible for them to recover except by a power greater than humankind, and that power was Jesus Christ. Jesus said, "I am the way the truth and the life, no man comes to the father but by me." (John 14:6 NKJV) The Bible states, if you repent and believe in Jesus and be baptized to receive the Holy Ghost you shall be saved. As the saying goes, I once was lost by now I'm found was blind but now I see."

God had to reestablish His kingdom through His Son, Jesus, because His kingdom through the first man, Adam, was lost and had to be found because Adam sinned, thereby creating a separation between God and humankind. That separation can be reestablished through our affiliation with God's Son, Jesus Christ. To be reattached to God, we must first accept His Son as the only way to receive salvation. Jesus said, "I am the true vine; you are the branches. He that abides in me and I in him the same shall bring forth much fruit" (John 15:1–5 KJV).

Whatever you ask in Jesus's name, the same shall be done unto you. You see, God promises us our hearts' desires, provided we remain in His Son, Jesus Christ. In fact, He promises us our hearts' desires as a reward for remaining righteous and abiding in Jesus and Jesus in us. Read John 15.

The kingdom of God is in each of us via our relationship with Jesus, the intercessor between humankind and God. Jesus preached the gospel of the kingdom in three simple steps:

1. Repent and believe the gospel of Jesus, along with the death, burial, and resurrection of Jesus.
2. Be baptized with the Holy Ghost.
3. Become fishers of people to draw all people unto Him.

Your ultimate goal, or your job, is to become a disciple of Jesus by attempting to draw all people unto Jesus Christ, for out of the abundance of the heart, the mouth speaks. Be careful to speak the true doctrine of Jesus, for if the heart is right, the mouth will speak the true doctrine of Jesus. For if the heart is right, the mouth will speak of the righteousness of God. Go ye therefore into all the world and preach the gospel to every creature. He that believes and is baptized shall be saved, but he that believes not shall be damned. God is looking for fishers of humankind. Will you become one?

God's Plan for Humankind Is to Prosper, Provided They Are in the Delight of the Lord

"Blessed is the man that walks not in the counsel of the ungodly, nor stand in the way of sinners, not sit in the seat of the scornful. But the delight is in the law of the Lord; and in his law does he meditate day and night. And he shall be like a tree planted by the water that bring forth his fruit in his season; his leaf shall not wither and whatsoever he does shall prosper. The ungodly are not so but are like the chaff that the wind drives away. Therefore, the ungodly shall not stand in the Judgement, not sinners in the congregation of the righteous. For the Lord knows that ways of the righteous; but the way of the ungodly shall perish." (Psalms 1:1-6 KJV).

Let us examine the paragraph. "The counsel of the ungodly" means that you should not hang out or be in the company or assembly of sinners because the devil controls sinners and sinners have a way of changing you to conform to their ways. Sinners work against God and are therefore ungodly.

If you are a Christian, you need to hang out with Christians. "The seat of the scornful" refers to people who hold others in extreme contempt. They despise others, disregard others, or totally ignore others. If you are a Christian, you should not hang out with the scornful but always try to hang out with other Christians. When you walk in the righteousness of the Lord, you will be blessed, and your blessings will not wither or fade away. You will always prosper because God has promised if you remain righteous, He will pour out blessings too numerous for you to comprehend.

In fact, He said, "Your leaves or your ways will not wither and whatever you do will prosper." The way of the righteous points to prosperity because God promised that you will always bear fruit in your season, your leaf will not wither, and whatever you do will prosper because He has ordained this to be so.

Let us look at all the great righteous men of the Bible, such as Abraham, Joseph, David, Solomon, Job, and so forth. All were righteous, and they were wealthy. Look at all great religious leaders, even those of the present. Chances are, if they are proven to be righteous, they are also very wealthy. Consider people such as Billy Graham, Pat Robinson, TD Jakes, and so on.

In fact, beginning with the first man, all Adam had to do was obey God, remain faithful and righteous toward God, and have dominion over everything that God had created. In essence, he would have been the wealthiest man of all time, but Adam failed and became ungodly by this very first act of disobedience. At this point, sin was introduced into the world. Humankind became ungodly by disobeying God and continues to do so even to this day.

Let us look at what happens to the ungodly. The Bible says the ungodly are like the chaff, which the wind drives away and therefore will not stand in the judgment. Nor will they sit in the congregation of the righteous because God knows the way of the righteous, but the way of the ungodly shall perish. In other words, the ungodly cannot enter into the kingdom of heaven because none but the pure of heart can walk up there, for the pure of heart shall see God.

Chaff is like the husk of corn or grass that can easily blow away, but the way of the righteous is like fine wine. It gets better with age with the final destination, heaven, where we want to make our home. Do you want to make heaven your home? If you do, you need to get your house in order because none but the pure of heart can walk up there. The road is broad, but the way to heaven is very narrow. I don't know about you, but I want to walk that narrow path, which leads to eternal life, because the way of the ungodly shall perish, but the way of the righteous shall prosper because God knows His sheep. His sheep call Him by His name. His name is Jesus.

If you want to get to heaven, you must call Him by His name. The name is Jesus. God promises us that if we remain faithful and follow Jesus, the Lord will order our steps and whatever we do shall prosper. The righteous will always be blessed, but the way of the ungodly shall perish. See Psalms 1 and 37.

God Resists the Proud but Gives Grace unto the Humble

"**B**lessed are the meek for they shall inherit the earth; and shall delight themselves in the abundance of peace," says Matthew 5:5 KJV and Psalm 37:11 KJV. You see, God has always intended for humans to be meek and humble in order for us to understand that we do not have any power other than that which God has given us.

When people start to believe that they have power and can control something, they deceive themselves. Even the greatest people ever created had to humble themselves before God. Let's look at Moses. God told him, "Take off your shoes because the ground you stand on is holy ground." In fact, God appeared to Moses in a burning bush because Moses was not worthy enough to look upon the face of God. In fact, no person is able to gaze upon the face of God because of the omnipotence of God, who is almighty with unlimited power.

Look at Paul. He was perhaps one of the greatest men created by God, but even he had a "thorn in his side." The devil is more powerful than humankind, but he must also answer to God. Look at (Job 1:6–11 KJV). "When he said to Satan, 'whenst comest thou?' Then Satan answered the Lord and said, 'I have been going to fro in the earth, and from walking up and down in it seeking whom I might devour.'"

You see, the devil can devour you, but even the devil has limitations. He must still answer to God. The devil is wiser than humankind is and can control a person's life, but God controls the devil. He only permits the devil to do what He will allow. God gave the devil power over Job, but he could not take Job's life. Only God has the right and power to take a person's life. A person takes lives every day by killing or through wars, but humankind does not have the right to take another life. People only have the power of God to allow it to happen.

Now let's look at the proud. Proud people are presumptuous. They take things for granted and are usually very arrogant. They are almost like the devil because they are selfish and believe in their own abilities. They are epic competitors and blessed with tremendous talent. They believe in their own self-worth without stopping to think that God gave them all of their abilities.

In fact, their lives can be changed within a matter of seconds. You could be in the right place at the wrong time when the bank is being robbed, and you could be shot and become paralyzed. You would not have gone to the bank at that time. You see, God can change things within a matter of seconds. Superman became a paraplegic just by falling off a horse.

The proud will fall because God cannot allow people to believe that they do not need God. When you never pray or go to church or believe in your own self-worth and abilities above and beyond the point where you become arrogant, you are setting yourself up to be resisted by God. Even when a person becomes great, to the point of being a monarch or a president, he or she must remain humble to receive God's favor. He or she can run for a long time but cannot outrun God. God said, "Every knee will bow and every tongue shall confess that I am God and there is none other than me." God said to Moses, "Tell them that I AM sent you."

You see, I don't care how proud or how great you are or even how good you look. God can do things that people cannot do. Within a matter of seconds, you could end up in jail for life for something that was not wrong. Nelson Mandela is a good example. He went to jail for something like forty years for protesting the inhumane treatment that Africans were receiving in South Africa, and after forty years, he was released and became the president of South Africa. Humility remained one of his greatest traits throughout this horrible ordeal and is perhaps one of the reasons why God bestowed favor upon him.

In fact, God promised to bestow favor upon the humble, going all the way back to the Israelites after they had wandered in the wilderness for forty years. Deuteronomy 8:16 states, "He fed them in the wilderness manna, which their fathers knew not, that he might humble them and they he might prove them to do good at their latter end."

You see, God promised to never leave them, provided they kept the commandments, remained humble, and believed that God's power sustained them during their forty years of wandering. In fact, when you read Deuteronomy 8, you will see that God's intentions were to humble them so they could never forget that they survived because of God's grace and mercy.

Even today God continues to give grace to the humble and resist the proud. We must always remember that it is because of the Lord's mercies that we are not consumed. Because His compassion fails not, they are new every morning. No matter who or what we are, if we remain humble, we will always operate under God's grace and always be blessed. Amen!

Healing the World

"There is healing for the soul," says the Lord is an expression that I have heard in church and through various biblical studies and is being used as an example to help clarify this subject matter. What is the meaning of this expression is difficult to explain? When we are able, to surmise its meaning, we may find answers to healing the world. Let us examine this popular saying. What is the soul? The soul is the mind or brain in the person's body. That component causes a person to know right from wrong or some variation of each or both. Humankind is number two in the scheme of things. God is number one.

When a person or the world, which is made up of humankind, accepts that they are number two and God is number one and allows God to control humankind instead of humans trying to control humankind through a combination of the church and the state or the government, only then will we be able to understand how to heal the world. There is healing for the world when we reinvent with the understanding that God is first in everything and allow God to control the world. Only then will we be able to heal the world.

The problem with the world is that people believe that they, instead of God, control it. It is true that humans had been given dominion over everything God created, but God is the Creator, and no person is greater than the Creator. We must understand that humankind is separated from God by the original sin of Adam. God constantly tried to reattach humankind to Him through all of the many prophets, judges, and kings He sent before He sent Jesus into the world to bring humans back to Him under His plan for salvation that was given to Jesus.

When a person truly accepts Jesus's teachings instead of a watered-down version of Jesus's teachings because it offends some variation of man-made laws made by the government and the church, only then will we be able to heal the world. Isaiah 1:15–31 KJV says it best.

> And when you spread forth your hands, I will hide mine eyes from you: when you make your prayers, I will not hear, your hands are full of blood. Wash you, make you clean, put away the evil of your doings from mine eyes, cease to do evil. Learn to do well; seek judgment, relieve the oppressed, judge the fatherless, plead for the widows. Come now, and let us reason together, saith the Lord: though your sins be as scarlet, they shall be as white as snow; though they be as red like crimson, they shall be as wool. If you are willing and obedient, you shall the good of the land, but if you refused and rebel you shall be devoured with the sword of the mouth of the Lord has spoken it.

This exchange was between God and humankind during the days of Isaiah. God was talking to Isaiah about the children of Israel. He was very angry at the return to God because they had become a disobedient and rebellious nation. God was forced to exercise His will to destroy them because of this, as stated in Isaiah 1:9: "Except the Lord of hosts had left unto us a small remnant." We should have been as Sodom, and we should have been like unto Gomorrah. But God is a patient God and has been reluctant to, totally, destroy humankind. He left a remnant to always allow us to return to Him.

This remnant remains to this day. He is always willing to give us another chance when we actively seek Him. He gave us another chance when He said, "I will turn my hand upon thee and will purely purge thee of thy dross which is defined as they waste and I will restore thy judges as at first and thy counselors as at the beginning after that, thou shall be called the city of the righteousness, the faithful city."

You see, Isaiah was describing a story of humankind's sins that had become so abundant that God considered destroying the world more than three hundred years before Christ was born. Each time He agreed to give humankind another chance by destroying almost all of humankind, He always relented and left behind a small remnant.

You see, God could have destroyed the entire world numerous times before He sent His Son to save us by sending His prophets to warn the people to repent and become reattached to Him, but unfortunately humankind never repented and remains separated even to this day. That remnant has evolved into what the world is about today. That faithful city of righteousness has never truly come into existence.

God continued over many generations to send additional prophets, judges, and kings, and finally as a last resort, He had to send His only begotten Son to give humankind a final chance to repent and become reattached to Him. Jesus is our final chance to become reattached to God. Through His grace and mercy, He can allow us to become reattached to God.

You see, through His grace, it allows Him to forgive us, and through His mercy, it allows Him to help us. The world can only become reattached to God when we give up all the things of the world and follow Jesus's teaching in its entirety, not a watered-down version.

The New Testament of our Lord and Savior Jesus Christ must become our sole foundation. The church and the state or the government must base all of their laws on the teachings of Jesus as the foundation of its thinking.

How to Be a Good Father

If you had to describe a good father, what is the first word that would come to mind? I would imagine things like a leader, provider, mentor, and a host of other words too numerous to mention. Unfortunately, the term *father* is used so loosely defined nowadays that it is difficult to quantify or describe what is its actual meaning. It certainly means a lot more than someone who fathered a child. We are living in a society composed of so many mothers in the role of a single parent. It is often hard to determine what happened to the fathers. Are they in jail, deceased, or just missing in action?

Suffice it to say, all of the preceding is true. Prisons are homes to a large percentage of the men who fathered a child. Many more are deceased from drugs, crime, and other deviant social discord, and the rest are just missing in action. They are fathers in body but not in the mind and deeds. Their children are left to care for single mothers and grandmothers. They are left on the welfare rolls and the streets while their fathers languish in some morbid state of self-exile. If this situation does not change, I am afraid our children are headed for self-destruction, doomed to become misfits and wards of society.

Young men who are responsible for fathering a child must become reliable, responsible, and accountable to ward off this pending catastrophe. A good father embodies the principles of reliability, responsibility, and accountability. These three principles, combined with a strong spiritual value system, are the key ingredients for being a good father. When a seventeen-year-old kid fathers a child, unless the mentality of abandonment stops, our children are doomed to failure.

Let's start by examining each of these principles for being a good father. Reliability stands for dependability. A good father can be depended or relied upon to perform certain deeds. A child or the child's mother should be able to depend upon the father to bring in the bacon for his family. They don't have to worry about the father going to Atlantic City every time he gets a paycheck to gamble away his earnings, leaving his family hungry and concerned about whether the rent is paid. They don't have to worry about the father chasing other women, spending his money on them while neglecting his children.

They don't have to be concerned about the father lying, cheating, and disrespecting his home, neighbors, and community. They don't have to worry about receiving a call in the middle of the night, saying the father was arrested for burglary or got caught selling drugs. They know they can depend on the father to provide leadership. They know they can depend upon the father to encourage his children to become self-sufficient and independent to work hard and go to church on Sundays.

They know they can always depend on the father to lead by example and deeds and not just by word of mouth. They know that whenever there is a crisis, the father is there to offer assistance. They don't have to worry about him being missing in action, being in jail, or running from his responsibility. They don't have to worry about the father having children all over town and denying they exist. They know he is committed to one family. We could go on and on, but it is not necessary to continue to know what is meant by reliability and dependability. It relates to being a good father and not just a man who helped a child to be born.

Now let us examine responsibility, which is intertwined with reliability. A responsible person is first and foremost trustworthy. He or she has the power to consult to make a decision. Responsible people are answerable for their and others' actions. A good father is responsible for his children, family, community, and country. The key thing here is that he must be of good character, sound mind, and excellent judgment to be held in high esteem so there is no question that he is concerned enough about himself, family, and neighbors to do what is best for all concerned.

When he needs to make a decision, it should be in the family's best interest, and it is not based on selfish motives. He can be trusted to be accountable for his and others' actions. A good father is slow to cast blame and quick to offer praise, but he must be firm and disciplined enough to discipline without being viewed as being harsh and excessive.

There are times when tough decisions must be made that may go against the children or concerned parties, but a good father knows best and must make those decisions under sometimes unfriendly circumstances. His commitment level must be beyond reproach. There are many times when you are forced to make decisions that your children and/or family may oppose, and you must hold firm in your convictions in spite of the indifferences.

For example, your son turns sixteen and wants you to buy him a car because the next-door neighbor's son was given a car when he turned sixteen. He tells you that you don't love him because you refused to buy the car. As a father, you must make an unfavorable decision because you know it is rare that a sixteen-year-old child is responsible enough to care for a car. In addition, you must explain to him that love is not based on giving material things. Know that this is the last thing he wants to hear.

Some fathers under these circumstances would give in and buy the car, knowing it is not the wise thing to do, but they want to remain friends. A good father sometimes must render difficult decisions even though he knows it is not favorable.

Accountability is closely related to responsibility. An accountable person is thrust in a position of having to possibly explain his actions. A good father is never afraid to explain his actions because his actions are based on doing the very best to satisfy his family. They don't have to worry why a decision was made. They know it was made in the best interest of all concerned parties.

Being accountable is being responsible and vice versa. A simple thing like telling your child that you will return to perform certain tasks and failing to do so could have a devasting effect on a child. A good father's world in his bond. If he made a commitment, then he keeps it.

He would never lie about it because it creates mistrust and deception. It is always better to tell the truth, even under unfavorable circumstances.

The last and final criteria for how to be a good father are based on a strong spiritual value system. Nothing is more important than having a strong spiritual value system. It does matter what religious affiliation you belong to. Every religion has some basis of goodness for humankind. A good father is rooted in the spirit of man. Unfortunately the body is made of flesh, and the flesh will sin, but the mind is rooted in the spirit. And through the spirit, you can receive redemption. As a good father, you should be on a solid foundation to live a righteous life and set a good example for your children.

If men are rooted in the spirit of humankind and the goodness of God, men and boys who are makers of babies would become fathers of babies. They would know from a spiritual perspective that if they have fathered a child, then they are responsible for that child in its entirety. This can only come from having a strong belief system in the spirit of humankind and the goodness of God. The Bible and all religious books should be at the forefront of every single family because it gives a family a foundation of goodness.

If they were strong believers, there would be a lot fewer boys making babies and leaving the infants stranded and not knowing who their fathers were. Love for fellow humans would be increased. Self-esteem would become prevalent in society. Children would feel good about themselves and would not have to ask, "Who is my father?" and "Where is my father?" There would be more men getting married to the women they impregnated instead of making babies all over the place and leaving them to become wards of society on welfare and in prison. You see, from the Spirit emanates love, and love must transcend the essence of being a good father. Above all, a good father loves his children as he does himself.

It is no longer fashionable to say, "This is my child." It is much more important to become reliable, responsible, and accountable for your children, so they look up to you and say, "I want to be just like him because he is my father." This will happen when young and older men take responsibility for their children and their children know their fathers are reliable and can be counted upon because they are deeply rooted in a power greater than humankind—the power of God Almighty.

How to Be a Role Model

A re famous people role models? I don't think so. I think of a role model as someone you know or at least have some affiliation with. Do you know Michael Jordan? If you know him or at least knew him before he became famous, then perhaps you could view him as your role model. In any event, I think of a role model as someone you can make some type of judgment about from being in his or her circle of association.

Using this interpretation, whom do you consider your role models, and just how do we become role models? These people closest to you would qualify as having the possibility of being role models simply because it is easiest for you to access their character. Therefore, the first possibility for role models would be your parents or other close relatives, followed by your teachers, counselors, bosses, religious leaders, friends, or other acquaintances. Unless someone like Michael Jordan, Bill Clinton, or some other famous person can get by this first hurdle, then it is unlikely that individual will be your role model.

Ideally, this is the perfect scenario. There is no one closer to you than your parents. Let us examine how your parents are your role models. The first thing to examine is their character. This is not only true for your parents but for all role models. Their character must be exemplary. Can an abusive parent have an exemplary character? Absolutely not. Any kind of abuse is harmful. Look at the things that can be abused, such as sex, drugs, or alcohol. Consider physical and mental abuse. There is no way you can be a role model if you engage in any sort of abuse.

How can you determine if a famous person falls into one of these categories? There is no real way that you can know this unless perhaps you heard or read it in the media. A famous person could be beating his wife's butt on a daily basis and you would not know it. Certainly, if you knew this, that person would not be your role model. Martin Luther King said it best: "Judge not by the color of a person skin but by the content of a person character." The content of a person's character is, therefore, the first criterion for being a good role model.

The second criterion for being a role model is based on the example set by a person. The motto of "doing as I say and not as I do" is definitely not the proverbial wisdom that should be expressed when you are living a life of unrighteousness. This is certainly true when you examine someone like a minister or a teacher. A child should be able to look at a minister or teacher and say, "I want to be just like him because it is obvious that he is living a righteous life and not one of deception and fraud."

It is very important for a role model to set a good example, especially when you are dealing with parents, teachers, and religious leaders. How can you respect a minister if you know he is a womanizer? Obviously you can't. I read an article some time ago commenting on numerous basketball players who had fathered many children from many different women and refused to acknowledge it or accept the responsibility for providing for them. Can you look at a person like this and say that he is a role model? Obviously you can't. Is this the correct example to set for future generations? Probably not. A role model is someone of exemplary character who sets an example that he or she would be proud for you to follow. The ideal candidate should be your mother or father.

The third criterion for being a role model is someone of high morality who lives a good Christian life. You would certainly think that the priest, rabbi, or minister would qualify as a role model. Many of them do, but unfortunately this is not always true. Many religious leaders lie, cheat, and steal just as much as anyone else. Some get caught, and you hear of their escapades on various occasions. The majority of them do have a high moral character and live a good Christian life, and you would be proud to consider them as role models.

Think of the ministers in your own church, how they rate in the role model department. Think of prominent members of your church, deacons, and members of the trustee board. Are they role models? I sure hope so. Many church members are not, however. Many can't wait to leave church on Sunday to get a drink, smoke a joint, and so on. Or they beat the crap out of their wives. Are they role models? Chances are, they are not.

Another example of how to be a role model is to be a facilitator of peace and a discourager of turmoil. Martin Luther King Jr. was a good example of this type of individual. Much to a lot of people's chagrin, he was a facilitator of peace to a fault. He totally believed in nonviolence to bring about constructive change as opposed to inciting violence and turmoil. In some circles, he was thought of as being an Uncle Tom and a poor example of a strong leader. I think he did more to bring about peace among all nations throughout the world than perhaps any leader of our time. In fact, I think he did more to facilitate peace among the white race even more so than the black race because he did not bend or break in his propensity for peace even under extreme circumstances. He was often jailed and endured tremendous hardships to foster this idea of peace among all people.

Even in death, his legacy for peace and tranquility continues to grow. I think white America began to see a whole new side of black people based on his strong belief that all people should be judged on the content of their character much more than anything else, and this goes for whites and blacks. Would you consider Martin Luther King Jr. a role model? Unfortunately he is deceased, but indeed he would have been an excellent role model.

Other strong criterion for how to be a role model is a strong commitment to the principles of responsibility and accountability. Good role models are very responsible and concerned about their families and fellow humans. They will take control of their lives and be good providers for their families to ensure that their lives are comfortable and rewarding. Their accountability should be beyond reproach. Their word should be their bond. If they agree to do something, there should never be any doubt that they will carry out their commitment. As far as their credit history, there should be a very strong commitment to pay their bills on time because good credit shows that a person is trustworthy and can be relied upon to do the correct thing for himself and his family.

The last and final criterion, in my opinion, for being a role model is to have a strong belief in obtaining a good education. It is important to believe that ignorance is bliss and knowledge is a uniting force in society because it creates a better person and enhances a better world. Why is there so much turmoil in the world? A lot of it is based on ignorance of a person's culture, customs, belief, and way of life. Often ignorance causes more turmoil in the world than perhaps anything else.

A good role model takes the initiative to find the commonality among different races of people. Once you begin to look at people based on what they are instead of who they are, you find that 90 percent of all people are good and the 10 percent who are bad should not be the justification for judging the 90 percent who are good. This analogy is probably true among every single race, creed, or nationality.

Unfortunately, because of ignorance, a few bad apples can spoil an entire barrel. Knowledge can, therefore, be the defining force that unites and binds all people. The more you know about a person, the better you are able to assess his or her character and deal with that person based on what he or she is instead of who he or she is. A good role model is so secure in his or her own morality that he or she is willing to look at all parameters to mend relationships to create a better world instead of focusing on differences among people, which can often create turmoil. In other words, good role models have the knowledge to change the things they can and the wisdom to know the things they have no control over. They know that the essence of knowledge is a good education.

When I think of role models, I must think in terms of ordinary folks whom I encounter on a daily basis, not celebrities that I only know from what I see on a movie or TV screen. You must view folks like your parents, teachers, doctors, aunts, and uncles as examples of role models. These are the folks whom you are able to assess their character and determine the examples they set, either positively or negatively. Unfortunately, basketball players, movie stars, and singers don't fall into this category, even the great Michael Jordan.

How to Buy and Sell Real Estate

There are generally four ways of getting wealthy in this country: buy and sell real estate, inherit wealth, invest in the stock market, and operate your own business. Almost all wealthy people either own real estate or have owned real estate in some capacity in the past. Real estate is definitely a great wealth-sustaining vehicle because the value rarely goes down. The chances are good that it will appreciate, especially if the location is good. The other great value in owning real estate is the tax savings.

Your monthly mortgage payment includes a substantial portion of interest and property taxes. These two items are fully tax deductible, which offers a tremendous cash bonus to the recipient when taxes are prepared. It is therefore very wise to own as much real estate as possible to now only make money on the appreciation but also on the reduction of taxes.

In this module, I will teach you a method of buying and selling real estate based on my years in the business as a real estate broker and real estate owner. Before you go out to purchase real estate, it is always is a good idea to know how much real estate you can afford to buy. One way to do this is to get preapproved for a mortgage prior to beginning the process. Many financial institutions will do this service for you. If you want a layperson's way to do it, generally a financial institution will give you a mortgage of approximately two-and-a-half times your yearly income if your credit is good.

Webster's dictionary defines real estate as land and whatever is attached, such as natural resources or buildings. Keeping this definition in mind, let us examine some of the techniques used to buy and sell real estate. Let us examine this venue by looking at the various steps in the process. The first step is the looking process. What do we look for? Location, location, location is the cure-all for the looking process. If the location is great, the chances are extremely good that you will make a lot of money from buying and holding on to real estate or selling it.

You see, the principle behind this is that it is very easy to fix a piece of property, but it is very difficult to fix the area where the property is located. Would you rather own a piece of property on Park Avenue in New York or the swamplands in Florida? Therefore, finding the right location for your venture is your prime concern because of the word *appreciation*.

The location can make or ruin a piece of property. You can take the exact same piece of property and put it in New City in Rockland County or the Bronx in New York City, and the price could vary as much as 50 percent. Just how do you determine the right location? Well, it matters whether you are looking for a place to live, establish a business, or expect to hold onto for a period of time and sell it. In any event, the same techniques come into play. These considerations are centered on safety, convenience, and accessibility. If it is a residence, then school carries tremendous weight as well as houses of worship, shopping, noise, pollution, and so on.

You can have the greatest house or business in the world, but if it is located at the top of a mountain and you can only get to it using a helicopter, then what's the use? When you are looking to make a purchase of real estate for whatever purpose, you need to do your homework, which starts with a full investigation of the area.

You can do this in any number of ways. The police department, the fire department, the ambulance corps, the school district, people and businesses in the area, and so on can give you a good lead into whether there are any problems.

One of the very best methods is to take frequent trips to the area at all times of the day and nights, weekends and holidays and especially in the summer when the children are out of school. I am sure there are many other techniques, but the techniques mentioned here can prove invaluable in your search for the right piece of property for your investment.

The looking process usually involves the purchase of real estate and is centered on things that you should do on a personal level. When you are looking to buy real estate, it is absolutely necessary to employ a realtor's services. Some of the advantages of using a realtor are the following: a realtor usually has customers who might be suited to your property, and they are in the business and know how to market the property based on price and other economic and social factors.

Once a buyer is secured, a realtor can arrange to finance through one of the many financial resources that they encounter in their daily operations. In addition, a realtor will work hard to facilitate the closing on terms that are convenient to all concerned parties because that is their method of getting paid. Most realtors are familiar with many of the tax laws and can be an invaluable consultant for tax purposes. Although buying and selling real estate can be done without the use of a realtor, it is highly recommended to use a realtor in addition to your own ability to know the particulars.

Once you have located the right property, you instruct your broker to make an offer. The broker will require you to complete and sign a document, usually referred to as a binder. The official name of this document is called a notice of purchase and acceptance. It is a written document indicating the amount you are willing to pay when you expect to complete contracts, closing, and occupancy dates as well as the contingencies, including obtaining a mortgage, home inspections, termite inspections, and/or radon inspections. An offer generally requires a good faith deposit to show that this is a serious offer.

The amount of the check is not standard in all states. It can be as little as $100 or up to 5 to 10 percent of the purchase price. If the offer is not acceptable, further negotiations are necessary to reach an agreement between the buyer and seller. If no agreement can be reached, the amount of the binder check is returned to the buyer. Once the buyer and seller agree on the terms, the buyer arranges for the necessary inspections and applies for a mortgage. On these terms, the buyer arranges for the necessary inspections and applies for a mortgage. The seller instructs their attorney to prepare the contract of sale based on the agreed-upon terms between the buyer and seller.

Although some states may or may not require the buyer to use an attorney, it is highly recommended to use one. The sales contract usually includes, among other things, the following information:

1. Purchase price
2. Mortgage contingency as far as times references for obtaining the mortgage and what happens if mortgage is not obtained in this time period
3. Title conveyance and quality of title
4. Itemized listing of personal property included in the sale of the property
5. Brokers involved in the process and attorneys representing the buyer and seller

The contracts are usually prepared within a few weeks and will require the buyer to sign and return them to the seller for the seller's signature. A complete set of contracts will be needed for mortgage approval. At the signing of the contract by the buyer, the down payment is required. It can range from a zero-down payment if the buyer is applying for a van mortgage, roughly 3 to 5 percent for a far mortgage, or 5 to 20 percent for a conventional mortgage.

The type of mortgage is usually indicated in the contracts because there are different aspects and time periods for each. Generally your realtor and loan officer will be very helpful in determining which type is best for you depending on your credit history, income, and monies on hand.

Obtaining a mortgage is difficult and usually time-consuming, especially if your credit is not very good. There are many different types of mortgages with varying amounts of cash and income requirements. The van and far are generally not as strict as your credit history. Since you are dealing with the government, there are certain requirements that may be slightly different from a conventional mortgage, and the chances are good that it will take longer to process a van or far mortgage because the government has its own set of rules.

Once your mortgage is approved, the last and final step in the process is the closing title. There are numerous costs associated with this step. Although some of this cost can be negotiated between the buyer and seller, it is generally the buyer's responsibility to pay a closing cost. The following information represents a synopsis of some of the costs associated with closing:

1. Point of loan or origination fees. A point is 1 percent of the mortgage amount. Points are often used to reduce the interest rates, but at the same time, it increases closing costs. A zero-point mortgage usually has a slightly higher interest rate than a one-, two-, or three-point mortgage.
2. Interest on the loan usually calculated covering the period from date of closing until end of month.
3. Title work, including the title search, title insurance, and recording of title. The title work is usually one of the largest aspects of closing costs.
4. Survey fees. If not recently surveyed, the lender or title insurance company will require a new survey of the property showing the location of the property, boundaries of the property and easements, and right of ways, additions or deletions to the property, and so on.
5. Recording fees. The buyer is usually responsible for paying the fee for legally recording the new deed and mortgage.
6. Adjustment costs. The buyer is usually required to reimburse the seller for any monies that were paid prior to closing. Usually prepaid property taxes fall into the category as well as tax escrows required by the lender.
7. Prepaid hazard insurance. Lenders often require a one-year paid-up hazard insurance policy at closing.
8. Attorney fees, including your own personal attorney and the bank's attorney, are paid by the buyer.

9. Inspections for termites, radon, and so forth are paid by the buyer.

There are other costs associated with closing costs that may vary from state to state, but on average, a buyer can expect to pay approximately 8 percent of the mortgage amount in addition to the down payment before taking occupancy to a piece of property.

As you can see, buying and selling real estate is a very long and tedious process and can be quite expensive; therefore, it is very important for you, as the ordinary layperson, to know as much as possible to reap the many rewards.

How to Check for Asbestos

Asbestos is a mineral fiber found in various rocks. Many older homes were built using asbestos in areas like appliances, ceilings, walls, pipe coverings, floor tiles, and sometimes roofing materials. The old, large heating systems were often covered with asbestos-containing materials. Asbestos was generally used for thermal insulation and in the ceiling and walls for fire protection. Asbestos is extremely fire-resistant and acts as a material of choice for builders in both residential and commercial buildings because of its thermal and fire-resistant abilities and ability to make building materials stronger.

The use of it in older homes was without reservation until it was discovered that it causes cancer of the lungs and stomach based on studies that were done with workers exposed to it in large degrees over an extended period of time. What happens with asbestos is that some asbestos materials break into tiny fibers that can float in the air, and once it is inhaled, they can become lodged for a long time in tissues found in the body.

After many years of ingesting and inhaling these tiny fibers, certain forms of cancer of the lung and stomach can develop. Ordinarily asbestos within itself is not a health risk. It becomes a health risk when asbestos is disturbed, causing fibers to be released into the air for the people to breathe. By disturbed, I mean chipped, flacked, or scraped off. This is much more prevalent with soft, crumbling materials containing asbestos, which can easily be released.

Unfortunately many people refuse to buy a house when it is determined that asbestos is present without realizing that unless it is disturbed and released into the air and it is breathed in for a very long period of time, there is no apparent danger. Under normal circumstances, most people exposed to small amounts of asbestos do not develop any health-related problems like cancer. The study was done on workers who had been exposed to asbestos over a period of many years, and it was found to have some health-related effects, especially in workers who were also cigarette smokers. A combination of asbestos and cigarette smoking was shown to cause a greater chance of developing lung cancer when compared to nonsmokers or workers exposed to asbestos by itself.

Now that we have examined a historical perspective on the medical effects of asbestos, let us turn our attention on how to check for asbestos in our homes. Under ordinary circumstances, it is often very difficult for an ordinary person to know if a material contains asbestos. The only real way of knowing is to consult with the product manufacturer, who may be able to help you based on the type of product, age, model number, and serial number. The best way, however, is to hire an experienced and qualified professional who can determine if asbestos is present in your home. This is especially true if you are looking to purchase a home built prior to 1950. The chances are good that if you purchase an older home, you will want to do some renovations. And before beginning any renovations, you need to know if asbestos exists because renovations will disturb and release it and you will become exposed to it.

If you purchase an older home and intend to renovate it, you should hire a qualified contractor who is experienced in working with asbestos. Once you have determined that asbestos exists in your home, it is best to leave it alone and hire a professional who can take samples properly and find the best and most efficient manner to remove it.

As I said before, if you intend to do any type of renovations in any area containing asbestos, make sure you seek qualified help to perform the services. For more information on asbestos analysis and removal activities, contact the asbestos coordinator in the EPA in your area. For the states of Alabama, Florida, Georgia, Kentucky, Mississippi,

North Carolina, South Carolina, and Tennessee, contact the asbestos coordinator at (404) 347-5014.

There are several places where asbestos has been found in your homes. Asbestos has been added to various floor tiles to make them stronger. It is also found in the backing on some vinyl sheet flooring and is often found in the tiles and backing with vinyl or some type of binder. Fibers can be released if the tiles are seriously damaged from things like sanding or cutting to make them fit. If you need to repair damaged tiles, it is better to place new tiles directly over the old.

Some walls and ceiling joints may be patched with asbestos-containing materials if manufactured prior to 1977. This practice was outlawed after 1977. If the material is in good shape, leave it alone. If you intend to do any type of sanding, scraping, or renovations, get professional help.

Other places where asbestos have been found in older homes are where woodburning stoves have been installed and where oil, coal, or woodburning furnaces have been installed. If you intend to do this type of changes to those arrangements, it is best to remove them or upgrade the system using a qualified professional.

In older homes usually built between 1920 and 1972, asbestos was commonly used as a covering for hot water and steam pipes to reduce heat loss and prevent protection for burns. Also during this time, older homes often used asbestos materials as insulation. Anytime you are doing any type of remodeling or upgrading in older homes, get professional help. If you don't have to renovate or remodel, leave it alone.

Remember, asbestos is harmful once it is disturbed and released into the air where it can be inhaled. Other areas that once had asbestos are roofing and siding shingles and sheets. There aren't any apparent dangers in those areas because they are outdoors and exposed to the atmosphere. Asbestos is much more dangerous when it inside and disturbed. Generally, if it is outside, there is no apparent danger, but however if the roofing and shingles are badly damaged and require replacement, get professional help.

In summary, asbestos is not a serious threat to us at present since it has been outlawed for use in home and building construction since

1977. If you buy a home built after 1977, there is really nothing to worry about as far as asbestos is concerned. Some of us who revel in some of the older homes only need to be concerned if we intend to remodel or renovate them. Under these circumstances, it is extremely important to find out if asbestos is present.

Once it is determined that it is present, the key thing is to leave it alone and do not attempt the renovations unless you are a qualified professional in identifying and removing asbestos. In any event, always remember the best course of action is to get professional help.

How to Check for Lead-Based Paint

L ead poisoning is a serious malady among a lot of children, especially children in poorer neighborhoods. It results from eating or ingesting lead-based paint. Many of the old homes and old tenement buildings were painted using lead-based paint, and as the walls begin to crumble and peel, the surfaces painted with lead paint pose a serious danger to children who eat or ingest the chippings. Lead-based paint is no longer used as a material for painting, so the problem is not nearly as severe as in the years prior to 1970. This problem, however, still seriously exists in the poorer rundown slum area of almost every major city and the country and rural areas as well.

Unfortunately many children in these poor areas are exposed to lead-based paint, and a lot of the children are developing lead poisoning from eating or ingesting the chips from the crumbling paint surfaces. In the module, I will attempt to assess some of the problems associated with lead poisoning from exposure to lead-based paint and how to deal with and recognize the symptoms of lead poisoning.

Before we get into lead poisoning, we need to examine the parameters surrounding lead-based paint, namely what to expect from exposure to lead-based paint and how to check and eradicate it once it has been found.

Lead is classified as a very heavy metal used in the construction industry mainly because of its strength and durability. It is considered almost indestructible, but it is known to be very toxic and very harmful when exposed to it, even in small quantities. It has been estimated that over 50 million homes in the United States contain lead-based paint in addition to the contamination from water, soil, and housewares. Lead is very much like asbestos in that it is not so harmful until it is disturbed, inhaled, and ingested.

Normally this occurrence may not be a problem with grown-ups because it is unlikely that grown-ups eat and ingest lead-based paint, but very young children, once they start to crawl and move around, tend to put almost anything and everything in their mouths. Serious problems can result from eating and ingesting lead in any amounts, especially in young children.

The thing to keep in mind is that a very large percentage of homes and apartment buildings built before 1978 contain lead-based paint. If you intend to buy a home built prior to 1978, it is wise to have some knowledge on how to deal with renovations and proper repair of surfaces containing lead-based paint. If you live in one of the older apartment buildings, a housing project, or some other organized housing development, you must be especially concerned about the dangers of paint peeling and chipping and should bring any problems to the attention of your property manager.

Now let us turn our attention to some of the effects of lead on humans to include adults and young children. Studies have shown that lead disrupts the formation of heme, the molecule in red blood cells. Heme, when combined with globin, forms hemoglobin, which is used to carry oxygen throughout the body. Large amounts of lead in the bloodstream can cause anemia, cardiovascular problems, and other serious ailments such as liver problems and difficulties with the body being able to detoxify itself.

Studies have further shown that lead has a serious effect on the nervous system in adults and children, causing problems with blood pressure and the ability to ambulate and communicate effectively. In young children, lead affects the intelligence and ability to develop strong motor skills and hinders development of their emotional growth.

As I said in the foregoing statements, eating and ingesting lead-based paint can cause lead poisoning. Some of the symptoms of lead poisoning are frequent stomachaches, vomiting, and and/or a tired feeling. If you are living under conditions that are conducive to lead-based paint and suspect lead poisoning, seek medical help. Remember to help eradicate lead poisoning. Follow the instructions outlined below:

1. Watch what your children put into their mouths.
2. Teach them not to eat paint chips or pieces of plaster.
3. Wash your children's hands thoroughly and often.
4. Use a damp mop or vacuum up paint chips and plaster; remove all loose particles from your walls, ceiling, doors, furniture, and so on.
5. Notify your management office or landlord if excessive amounts of paint peelings or plastering exist in your apartment.

If you live in an apartment that is thought to have lead-based paint or if you bought a house that was built prior to 1978, there are certain accepted methods for testing to determine the severity of the problem. Generally, there are three ways to check for lead in paint: chemical spot-test kits, fluorescence machines, and testing laboratories.

The least effective of these methods is the spot-test kits because they are not quite as accurate as large testing situations. The fluorescent machines are better than the spot-test kits. Professionals often use these machines for lead testing. They work on the principle for x-raying the affected surfaces in various locations and have the samples sent to a testing laboratory. This method is often not used because not only is it expensive, it is time-consuming.

Lab testing, however, is the most accurate of all the analytical methods. Under ordinary circumstances, the ordinary layperson can use the spot-test kit to check for lead if you are not faced with overly large areas. The kits generally use a solution of sodium sulfide, which is applied to be painted surface. Once it is applied, if lead is present, a specific color will appear.

The disadvantage of the kits is the inability of the chemical to penetrate more than one coat of paint. As we know in older homes and buildings, several layers of paint are usually present. As a result, this method is not very accurate under these circumstances. A better method would be the use of portable XRF machines, which can be brought to a home to take readings on almost any surface.

What the machines does is x-ray certain areas, measures the emission of radiation from the lead in the painted surface, and calculates the concentration of the lead contents. Usually these machines are reasonably priced and are more accurate than the spot-test chemical kit. As with lead abatement and eradication, this method is generally used as the preferred method of choice. Although the lab testing method is the very best, it is quite expensive and causes a delay while waiting for the results when time might be of the essence.

Once it had been determined that lead-based paint exists in your home or apartment, the best thing for you to do is turn the job over to a professional if you want the lead removed. If you live in an apartment, your management office, landlord, or property manager should be consulted. If you own your own home, the responsibility lies with you as the homeowner. Your goal, however, is to turn the job over to a professional who has the knowledge of how best to handle the situation. The following is three recommended methods for removing lead paint from household surfaces:

1. Heat guns, under restricted conditions
2. Chemical strippers, both solvent-based and caustic
3. HEPA filter sanding under highly restricted conditions

Each of these recommended methods can be used on certain materials from wood to metal to marble. Of the three methods, chemical strippers and heat guns can be used on almost any substance. HEPA filter requires special handling and specialized equipment and are used on certain surfaces under controlled conditions. Ordinarily, it should be done by a qualified professional, as with all the other methods.

The following table is inserted verbatim, as in the illustrative comparison of on-site lead paint removal methods. A lot of the materials used for the preparation of this module are based on the book written by Laurence Faraday, entitled residential lead abatement. The writer takes no responsibility for the use of these methods and the materials thereof. This module is intended for instructional purposes only.

As we summarize, we must keep a few pointers in mind, and lead-based paint can be very harmful to your health and even more harmful to your children's health. If you suspect that lead-based paint is used in your living environment, it is generally not harmful unless it is disturbed, eaten, or ingested. If you suspect that lead exists, there are three methods to test for its presence and three methods used to remove it from painted surfaces.

The preceding paragraphs give you a synopsis of each method. If you want a very thorough knowledge of the entire lead abatement process, get Laurence Faraday's book at your local library. The key things are to pay attention to your children, watch what they put into their mouths, and get medical help if you suspect lead poisoning. Remember you, as an ordinary layperson, are not a professional. Consult with a professional if you need help with lead identification and lead removal. Good luck.

How to Do Your Own Tax Returns

W hy do most people do their own tax returns? We can thing of many reasons for this phobia. The chief reason is probably fear of the IRS. I am sure you have seen those movies about the life of Al Capone who was thought of as being an invincible gangster. People believe that if the IRS could bring down Al Capone, then certainly "little old me" would not have a chance. Perhaps you are right, but however, "little old you" tax returns are so simple that an ordinary layperson could do them. If you can read and follow simple instructions, "little old you" could do your own tax returns, which happens to be very legal.

The majority of families do not itemize deductions and can qualify to file a short form 1040A for your federal tax return. This form is not difficult to complete accurately if you are able to read and then follow some simple instructions and fill in blank spaces that apply to you. Blank spaces that don't apply to you can be left blank. This is really as simple as it gets.

The same is true for a lot of the other forms, including form 1040, federal tax return, or earned income credit (EIC) (1040A or 1040). We look at these forms and automatically know that we cannot complete them without realizing that this is entirely not true. You must realize that I am not advocating that you should not get professional help in doing your tax returns. In fact, I would recommend that you do so. I am only advocating that you can do your own tax returns without the use of a professional if you choose to do so.

In this module, I will go through various steps for you to take to complete your tax returns as accurately as a professional to avoid any delays in your refund. You will learn definitions like dependents, exemptions, credit, deductions, taxable income, earned income credits, itemized deductions, and standard deductions as well as the differences therein. I will also walk through completing form 1040, the longest and most complicated form to complete. If you are able to complete form 1040, the simplest form, 1040A, will be very easy. A lot of the information I will talk about can be found in publication 17, a free publication that anyone can pick up at your local IRS office that issues tax forms.

Completing your own tax return involves a planning process. You begin by:

1. Getting all of your records together for income and expenses (e.g., your W-2, interest and dividend incomes, pensions, incomes, social security incomes, and all other incomes from all sources). Once you work on income, you go to your expenses, for example, church payments, union dues, mortgages and tax payments, medical and dental expenses, and so forth. Credit cards are no longer considered as a deduction. Remember, the average family will not need to itemize deductions and therefore can complete a simple federal form, 1040A. The state and municipal forms differ slightly from state to state, but they follow the same general guidelines as the federal. Once you are able to do the federal forms, then state forms are generally easier.

2. Getting all forms with instructions, schedules, instructions, books, and publications that you need. Usually the IRS sends each family an income tax package with all of the forms that are normally needed by that individual family depending on how you generally file your taxes.

3. Filling your return using the materials that you have gathered.

4. Checking all of your fill-ins to ensure you have not made a mistake to avoid delays in your return.
5. Signing and dating your return.
6. Attaching all required forms and schedules.

The foregoing represents a brief synopsis of the tax return proceeds. Completing the actual return, however, is another story all together. The only way we can learn how to do it is to let us start by examining an ordinary tax return for Joe and Mary Blow. Joe works and earned $26,000. Mary works and earned $19,440. They have a small savings account and receive $70 in bank interest. They live in an apartment and pay $750 per month for rent. They have charge cards, store cards, and other credit cards showing they paid $1,275 in interest and finance charges for the year. They both like to go to church and paid out $3,600 in church dues, and they contributed $1,000 to their favorite charity. In addition, they were not reimbursed for $1,200 in medical and dental expenses. The W-2s for Joe and Mary combined indicates that $5,270 in federal taxes were withheld from their wages. This example represents "little old you." What do you do using the enclosed tax return form?

You will notice that I selected form 1040 as the individual federal income tax return for 1998. The year does not really matter. Each year the form is practically the same. The very first part of the form is shown as "label." The IRS usually sends you a set of income tax forms along with instruction books and the label to use for filing your return. It is normally found on the front of the book. You can peel off the label and attach it here, provided the information on the label is correct. In any event, your name, address, and social security number go into this area.

The second part of the form is shown as "filing status." Five different filing statuses are shown: single, married filing joint return (even if only one have income), married filing separate return, head of household (with qualifying person), and qualifying widow and widower. Let us examine each of these.

Single means it is only one person, who is usually not married. This box would be checked if it applies. Married filing joint return means even if only one person had income. This box would be checked if it applies. Note: Married filing a joint return usually allows you to pay fewer taxes than if you were married filing separate returns. This is a key difference between filing state two and three filing status.

Head of household applies when you are considered unmarried on the last day of the year. Note: You could have been married and separated or gotten a divorce. The second criterion for head of household is that you must have paid more than half the cost of keeping up a residence for you and a qualifying person for more than half the year. A qualifying person is usually your child who is single or your grandchild or adopted child. A married child can qualify under certain circumstances, one of which if the married child is your dependent. You can also qualify for head of household if the qualifying child is your child but not your dependent.

In this case, the child's name must be inserted on the line requesting this information. Head of household status can also be used if the qualifying person is your relative and you can claim the relative as a dependent.

Qualifying widow or widower is used when your spouse dies and you have a dependent child. You can normally use this filing status for two years following the year of the death of your spouse. What it allows you to do is to be taxed based on a joint return and use a higher standard deduction. Under normal circumstances, filing status one, two, three, and four applies to the average person. The best filing status would be two and five, if you qualify. Generally you pay fewer taxes with these two statues. Single and married filing separately generally pays more taxes. Head of household is better than either single or married filing separately but not as good as married filing jointly or qualifying widower. Remember, your filing status is based on your own particular circumstances.

The next part of form 1040 is classified as "exemptions," which are usually broken down into personal exemptions and exemptions based on dependents. Exemptions allow you to reduce your gross income to arrive at a taxable income. It works in a similar manner to a deduction, which also allows you to reduce your gross income to arrive at a taxable income. The federal government sets the amount of each exemption.

For the year 1998, set our exemptions and dependents as $2,700. You and your spouse are classified as your dependency exemptions. In this example, you can check a box for yourself, your spouse, and each of your dependents who do or do not live with you. To qualify as a dependent, the following criteria must apply:

- The person is a member of your household for the entire year or related to you.
- The person must be an US citizen or a resident of Canada or Mexico for any part of the tax year.
- You must have provided more than half of the person's total support for the year.
- The person must have gross income not greater than $2,500 during the year.
- The person must have been your child under nineteen years of age at the end of the year or under twenty-four years of age and a full-time student for any part of the year. Note: The person must always be related to you but is not required to live in your household for the entire year. For example, your child could be away in school for part of the year.

For the purposes of this example, an exemption is claimed for yourself, one for your spouse, and two for your children who live with you, for a total of four exemptions at $2,700 equaling $10,800.

The next part of form 1040 deals with income. In the example cited involving the Joe Blow family, line 7 would be shown as $45,550 ($26,000 + $19,550). Line 8A would be shown as $70. Schedule B would not apply because it is used when interest or dividend totals more $400.

Line 9 is left blank. (This line is used if the family received dividend usually from stocks.) Line 10 is left blank. (If you itemized deductions and received a state tax refund, then this amount would be entered.) Line 11 is left blank because alimony is connected with a divorce.

Line 12 is left blank. (If the Joe Blow family receives income or had a loss from their own side business, then Schedule C would be completed, and the results would be entered here.) Line 13 is left blank because it concerns whether you own stocks and bonds and then sold them and received a profit or loss.

Line 14 is left blank. (They do not invest in securities.) Lines 15A and 15B are left blank unless you had received some money from an IRA distribution. Line 16A and 16B are left blank. (They are used if you are receiving a retirement pension or annuity or borrowed some money from your pension.)

Line 17 is left blank. (It is used if you owned rental property or were involved in certain types of investments.) Line 18 is left blank. (If is used if you are a farmer and had some type of farm income.)

Line 19, unemployment insurance, is left blank. (It would have been used if either Joe or Mary Blow were unemployed and received unemployment insurance, which is considered income for tax purposes.) Line 20A and 20B is left blank. (It would have been used if either Joe or Mary Blow were receiving Social Security income.) Under certain circumstances, Social Security income is taxable.

Line 21 is left blank. It is rarely used but would be utilized for something that is out of the ordinary and cannot be listed in the foregoing. Line 22 is the total of everything listed from line 7 through line 21. In this example, the amount entered for the Joe Blow family would be $45,620 ($45,550 = $70). In this example, you can see that the total family income before deductions and exemptions is $45,620.

At this point, you are ready to find out if you will receive a tax refund. Let us proceed so we can find out.

The next part of form 1040 deals with adjusted gross income. Lines 23 through 32 are left blank. These lines are self-explanatory and would be filled in if they applied. Since they total zero, line 33 is the same as line 22, which would be shown as $45,620.

From this point on, we get into the meat and potatoes (computing taxes and credit using deductions, exemptions, and credits such as childcare). Line 34 is the same amount as line 33 and would be shown as $45,620. Lines 35A and 35B are left blank since they deal with being sixty-five years old or blind. (Joe and Mary are not sixty-five. Nor are they blind.)

In line 36, enter the larger of your deductions or standard deductions. Here you need to know the difference between the two before you can enter an amount. Generally your standard deduction is higher than your itemized deductions if you are a non-homeowner or own some type of real estate that you are paying a mortgage and property taxes on unless you had some extremely high medical and dental expenses that you were not reimbursed for. Credit card interest and finance charges are not tax deductible.

In any event to see which is higher, complete schedule form 1040 and compare the two amounts. Before you even prepare Schedule A, let us calculate a rough estimate of Joe Blow's deductions using the example given in the beginning exercise. If you add in the church dues of $3,600, the charity contributions of $1,000, and the $1,200 for medical and dental expenses, this amount would come to $5,800. In fact, this deduction of $5,800 would be even less because of medical and dental expenses, and insurance must total more than 7.5 percent of their gross income before it would have counted as a deduction.

In this case, the standard deduction of $7,100 for married filing jointly is higher because Joe Blow is not a homeowner and did not have any unusual medical or dental expenses. The standard deduction is a set amount determined by your filing status. Itemized deductions can be greater and have no limits except the limits established through the completion of Schedule A, provided you can prove these deductions exist through bills and receipts.

Ordinarily if you are not a homeowner, the standard deduction is greater for an average family, especially since credit cards and other charge card interest and finance charges are no longer tax deductible. On line 36, insert $7,100 based on filing status of married filing jointly. If you are single, the standard deduction would be $4,250. Head of household would be $6,250, and married filing separately would be $3,550.

Line 37 indicates to subtract line 36 from line 34, and in doing so, you would insert $38,520. Line 38 indicates if line 34 is $93,400 or less, multiply $2,700 times the number of exemptions claimed on line 6D. In this case, $2,700 times four equals $10,800.

Line 39 indicates taxable income. This means to subtract line 38 from line 37, yielding $27,720. Note: You have now computed the figure that you will use to compute the amount of tax owed to the government.

This figure is much less than your original gross income. To get your taxable income, you subtract your standard deduction or your itemized deduction from your adjusted gross income, and then you subtract the dollar amount of your exemptions. As you can see, deductions and exemptions are key ingredients that are needed to find your taxable income. The more of these two ingredients, the less your taxable income.

In line 40, using the tax tables, find your tax based on a taxable income of $27,720 using married filing jointly. In this example, your tax liability is $4,159. This amount would be compared to the amount of taxes withheld on your W-2 for you and your spouse to see if there is a refund due you or you owe more money to the IRS. In this example, we indicated that $5,270 was withheld from Joe Blow and his family. Before we can determine the exact amount, we must continue with the remaining parts of the form.

Lines 41 through 47 deal with certain credits. The key thing about a credit is that credits reduce the amount of your taxes, whereas deductions and exemptions reduce the amount to your gross income before your taxes are computed. Line 41 deals with child and under thirteen for which you are paying childcare expenses, like a daycare center. If this applies, you must complete and attach form 2441 to receive the credit. Lines 42 through 48 is credit that generally does not apply to most families. If they do, however, please get the proper information for claiming them. In line 49, from line 40, it yields the same $4,159.

Lines 50 through 56 deal with other taxes such as self-employment taxes. Normally none of this applies to most families. If it does, however, get the proper forms and complete as necessary. Lines 57 through 64 deal with the taxes that were withheld from your W-2. This forms the basis to determine if you receive a refund, if too much were withheld, and the amount you owe if too little were withheld.

In this example, $5,270 was withheld, which would yield a refund of $1,111 before any further credits. None of these other credits would apply to the average family, except possibly line 59A, which concerns earned income credit, and possibly line 60, which talks about additional child tax credit. The things that are important is line 59A, earned income credit. This credit can be as much as approximately $3,000 if you have two or more qualifying children and approximately $2,100 if you have at least one qualifying child. The maximum income to qualify for this credit is approximately $27,000. These figures are approximate because they can change from year to year.

In any event, if your gross income is less than $30,000 and you have at least one child under nineteen or under twenty-four (if a full-time student), you should check to see if you qualify by completing the worksheet and schedule, especially on earned income credit. In this example, Joe Blow would not have qualified because their gross income is well in excess of approximately $30,000. This earned income credit is very important for single mothers with one or more children because oftentimes their income is less than $30,000 and the refund, even if no taxes were withheld from you.

Lines 65 through 68 deals with the amount of your refund if you overpaid and the amount you owe if you underpaid. In this example after completing the entire form, the Joe Blow family is due a tax refund of $1,111.

The final step in the process of completing your own tax return is to review everything to see if you made any errors. If you did not, both you and your wife should sign the form and mail them, along with copies of all attachments, to the IRS office shown in the income tax package for your area if you did not receive mailing envelopes for your use.

The intent of this module is to give the average person an opportunity to complete their own tax returns. As I said, it is not intended to replace professional help that you may need. By all means, if you need professional help, get it.

How to Establish a Website

It is almost impossible to market your business whether it is a product or service business without the use of the internet. There is truly a fallacy when entrepreneurs believe that if they have the greatest product in the world, someone will beat a path to their door to buy that product. So there must be a demand for it because the greatest product in the world cannot be sold unless you create a demand for it. The public will not beat a path to your door; you must forge a path to the public using various marketing techniques.

The internet in the last several years has become the number-one source of getting your product to the public. In this module, I will attempt to show you how to establish a website on the internet to create the demand for your business. We will examine terms like merchant accounts, links to other accounts making money with email, establishing a commercial website, joint ventures, power publishing, and the training, all necessary to market your product.

One of the first things you do to create a website is to establish a merchant account. What it does is allow you to receive payments for your product or services by a buyer using his credit card in a very secured setting to make purchases on the internet. One of the greatest fears of a prospective buyer is that his or her credit card, once it is made public, can be illegally used by an unscrupulous person or some hacker to make purchases that a buyer is not aware of.

As an entrepreneur, you must assure the public that the use of a buyer's credit card is strictly confidential and there is no fear that it can be used by a crook because of various security codes and other steps taken to prevent this from happening. The way a merchant account works is that a person who lands on your website will be able to peruse your site to make purchases, and once a decision is made to purchase, that person will be transferred to another account via a technique called linking, in which they will not be able to process with the purchase until a method of payment is made. Various methods of payments may be done via the use of a credit or debit card to finalize the purchase. The process of transferring somewhere else on the internet is called linking.

Now that we have examined how to get paid on the internet, let us process how to establish a website but, more importantly, how to make money from the establishment of your website. You must understand that the mere establishment of a website does not guarantee that you will make money. There are millions of websites on the internet that are not making any money at all. It is not that the product of service might not be great, but if no one is beating a path to your door, there is no money to be made. The only person that made money is the person you paid to establish your website.

Unfortunately, there is a fallacy that once you establish a website, you sit on the beach and wait for the money to roll in. This is far from the truth. Think about this. If there are millions—or perhaps billions—of websites, what are the chances that someone will stop on your website and will want to buy your product once they get there? The chances are a million (or billion) to one. Your goal is to get someone or a least as many people as possible to stop on your website. The more the merrier. Just how is this done? You must understand that websites by themselves do not make money.

This establishment of a website for business purposes is often referred to as a commercial website or storefront. It is used to market goods or services or a combination of the two to be made accessible to the public twenty-four hours per day. How is it done is the key. There are generally three methods for creating a website:

1. Do it yourself on your own computer.
2. Lease space on someone else's computer.
3. Place your storefront in an electronic mall.

Let us know examine each method. The first method of doing it yourself can be done, but it is not recommended. The fallacy of doing it yourself will allow you to have one of the million or perhaps billions of websites that are established that no one visits because you don't know what you are doing. In addition, you don't have a clue what is required to get someone to stop on your website. It is just like building a house. You can build a house yourself or hire a professional. You can fix your own electricity and blow up this place or hire a professional. You can fix your own plumbing and flood the basement or hire a plumber.

The second method is also not advisable because there is no guarantee that placing your website on someone else's computer will generate income for you because they very well may not know how to market your product. You see a website by itself is not a cure-all for making money. You do want to make money, don't you?

The third and best method to establish a commercial website is to use the services of a professional. You can find professionals listed in your local telephone directory, but the key thing they will do, besides charging you an outrageous fee, is to set up a website that will join millions and perhaps billions of other websites that no one visits and as a result makes no one money.

Several publications list the best and more well-known electronic malls. The one I have had success with is Galaxy Mall Inc., a publicly traded company on the over-the-counter market using the ticker symbol (glxy). Setting up a website is not cheap, so it is important to know what you will receive for your investment. Fees can range to upwards of $2,500 or more for just the programming and setup fee. Usually there is also a maintenance fee associated with a company if you want to remain affiliated with them through the use of their training materials. These fees can range to upwards of approximately $1,000 or more. The key again is to know what you receive for your money because a website by itself is not the key to making money. You need the tools, just like a mechanic needs tools to fix your car.

Galaxy Mall Inc. is famous for providing the tools for you to become successful because your success helps to ensure their success through a continuing affiliation with their company. They help to provide the tools through their extensive training program where you learn how to market your product on the internet. They learned years ago that the establishment of a website is a total waste, if you don't receive any hits on it. To ensure that you receive some of the 10 to 13 million hits per month in the Galaxy Mall, they teach you various marketing strategies, such as "How can I get to the top of the many search engines used to traverse the millions of websites on the internet?"

You see, unless your company is listed within the top ten or so companies in your specialty, there is very little chance that your company will be visited by the billions of people who surf the internet, and as a result, you will not make money, and there will not be a need for their services through an annual maintenance agreement. One of the keys to the success of your website is to be visited on a regular basis.

Galaxy Mall helps to ensure that this happens through their extensive training program on how to make money on the correct use of emails by not sending it to everyone but concentrating on a specific target group and how to make money using some of their thousands of mailing lists as well as growing your business through the use of joint ventures and power publishing. The use of these specialized marketing tools will not only help you to get to the top, but over the top. So it is essential that you learn how to use them by attending the workshops that are set up in various locations throughout the country. Knowledge is power, and unless you know what you are doing, it is impossible to become successful.

Unless you are a merchant already established with Galaxy Mall, it is difficult to get the information necessary to attend the workshops. The best methods are to use the services of an established merchant to be the go-between to get you started in establishing your own personalized website. In fact, it is usually cheaper if you use this method. An established merchant is somewhat like a broker who can bring the two parties together.

In addition, you may be able to form a joint venture with the established merchant, which can allow you to sell your product without incurring the expense of establishing your own personalized website. To obtain further information, please send your email request to trem1944@gmail.com.

As you can see, the mere establishment of a website is not the key to your success. Unfortunately knowledge plays a very important role. The more knowledge you gain on how to effectively market your product on the internet is the key to whether you remain a secret agent or an agent who is used over and over again and makes money repeatedly. You must take action to change your future because the definition of a fool is someone who continues to do the same thing over and over, expecting different results.

The internet is the key for growing your business, but unless it is used properly, you will have a deadbeat website that only you visit. Don't let this happen to you. Get the help you need to become successful, or you will remain a fool. Contact Tom Rembert Jr. via email at trem1944@ gmail.com. Please don't wait! Do it now!

How to Establish Good Credit

Credit is the foundation of all monetary systems. Without credit, it is almost impossible for a monetary system to exist. Business can be defined as buying and selling goods and services. Think about being able to perform this function without credit. There is no way you can pay for everything with cash or better. What is the first thing that an MBA graduate from Stanford looks for? I would say a venture capitalist comes to mind. These rich folks like Warren Buffet have financial companies set up to finance some clever product or idea that these MBA candidates espouse. These smart kids are looking to borrow to finance their product or idea, and venture capitalists are there to loan them the money.

After they obtain financing, they file an IPO and get rich from some dot com company. You see, credit is the foundation of the universe. The United States borrows from Japan, and Japan borrows from the United States. A company selling stocks is a company borrowing money. You buying a car is you borrowing money. Without some form of credit, most financial transactions would not occur in this or any country. You can get rich with good credit and go into the gutter without it. Therefore, it is very important for an individual to have good credit. In this module, I will teach you how to establish good credit, and once there, I will show you how to maintain it.

Do you realize that credit card companies are the greatest asset for establishing good credit and the greatest liability for ruining it?

Think about college students. It appears that the first thing that these credit card companies do is give a college student a credit card. What happens with this procedure can be a great benefit to this student or the ruination of their future. It becomes a matter of choices. The average person—and certainly a seventeen- or eighteen-year-old kid—all use a credit card if they receive it. This is when the choices come into play. You can pay the bills and establish good credit or don't pay the bills and establish poor credit.

I remember hearing somewhere that about 60 percent of college students have bad or poor credit upon graduation, either from credits cards, cellular phones, or beepers. This is a staggering statistic. If parents did not bail out many of these students, this percentage would be much higher. So the immediate priority becomes how to establish good credit, especially if you have none.

This first step in establishing good credit is to open a savings account at your local bank. Your immediate goal in doing this is to establish collateral. Think in terms of thousands. Get the first thousand, and more thousands will come to you either from borrowing or interest. When you have collateral, it is much easier for a lender to talk to you. You don't have to think in terms of your local banks, credit unions, stockbrokers, credit card companies, and so forth.

The point I am trying to make is that lenders will listen when you carry a big stick like collateral. Money talks, and bullshit walks. Once you have established at least $1,000 in collateral, you are ready to go the second step in establishing good credit to establish a good reason for obtaining a loan. I used the bank for this example because the bank is like your neighbor. They know you, and you know them from transacting your business with them, like cashing a check, paying bills, depositing money, and so on.

It is much easier to do business with someone you know and more importantly someone who knows you. They know whether you are bouncing checks every week, taking money out of the bank as soon as it is put in, or fighting with the teller every time you come in. In other words, you are not creating problems for them. They can count on your little money remaining in the bank so they can use it to make money for themselves, which is what they do with your money.

The good reason for getting a loan is for good paper, one that make sense to the bank, not necessarily you. You can't use things like "I want a loan to buy my girlfriend a leather coat." Suppose, however, you just started a new job requiring you to commute, and the easiest way for you to commute is the use of a car. Then a car loan might be a good reason for a loan. It makes paper sense. They don't come back in a few weeks wanting to see the car you brought or the paralegal registration. What you actually did with the money is not a major concern of the bank. It is more important for you to have a good reason for the loan and even more important that you pay it back.

The third step in establishing good credit is to use your collateral and good reason and go to your loan officer for a loan. If you don't have credit at all, this is an excellent way to establish credit. If you saved $1,000 and have it linked to your savings account, you are using your collateral to get the loan. The chances are excellent that you will get the loan if you can show there is a reasonable chance that you can pay it back.

If not, the bank has your collateral in reserve. Once you get the loan immediately, open up a checking account that uses the proceeds from the loan. One week before the payment is due, make monthly payments every month until you pay back the loan. You will notice that you are not making payments from your own funds. You are making them use the proceeds from the loan. If you can do this at several locations, you will be joining an elite class, a class of individuals with grade-A credit.

This simple technique can open the door for more credit than you will ever need. You don't ever have to go back to those lending institutions. They will come to you, trying to get you to borrow more and more money. Once you establish good credit, you can buy anything in this country that you want using credit. Financing ventures using borrowed funds is known as using the system of leverage. This system allows you to use as little of your own personal money as possible to buy as much goods and services as possible.

Donald Trump, before he became president, was perhaps the master of this system. Some large financial institution was always willing to finance one of his ventures. I imagine he used very little of his own personal money to build places like the Taj Mahal, Trump Towers, and so forth. How many financial institutions would say no to Donald Trump? If he decides to file bankruptcy, he can bankrupt possibly several banks. Just not paying some of his loans can be detrimental to many banks.

The last and final step in establishing good credit is to pay back what you borrowed in regular intervals during the time periods that you agreed to pay it back. This sounds very simple, but it appears to be the hardest thing do. How many people do you know say, "Because I paid more than what was due last month, it is okay for me not to pay anything this month"? Well, if you use this system, you are setting yourself up for failure.

Lending institutions don't want casual and sporadic payments, no matter whether they are large this month and none the next month or a little this month and none for a few months. They want you to pay within the required time and at least the minimum payment or more than the amount that is due. The rule of thumb is to pay the amount owed on or before the date that it is due. If you do this always, you will rarely be turned down for a loan that you can afford to pay back based on your income.

Maintaining good credit is using the same principles for establishing good credit. Once you obtain credit, you can maintain it in several factors centered around paying on time or not. When you always pay on time and pay off loans on or before it's due, you will be classified as having excellent credit.

Credit institutions use a system of credit reporting agencies to determine your credit worthiness. The three most prominent credit reporting agencies are Experian, Equifax, and Transunion. All lending institution subscribe to at least one or all of these three reporting agencies. Your credit worthiness is based on a system set up to provide scores on how you make payments, for instance, within the time allotted, thirty days late, sixty days late, ninety days late, collection account, charge-off, judgments, foreclosure, and bankruptcies.

Depending on your score using these parameters gives a lending institution a reason to accept or reject your request for a loan, credit card, mortgage, and so on. Your goal is to have excellent credit by always paying your bills on time, not just some bills but all. If you are forced to pay late a few times, never pay more than thirty days late. A few thirty days will classify you as B or C credit. Anything beyond that, like sixties, nineties, or worse, you are setting yourself up for failure in life. Without decent credit, there is very little chance of you becoming successful until you repair your credit.

In one of my other modules, I will teach you how to repair bad credit. It is your goal, however, to never get to this point. Remember, you can obtain pretty much anything in life by establishing good credit and maintaining it. You should always think about this when you get these tempting offers to get this and that type of credit card. Look at your budget and ask, "Will I be able to pay this bill on time every month until it is paid off?" Unfortunately, credit cards are rarely paid off.

How to Get a Job

The most important thing that everyone needs for good self-esteem is to have a good job that is satisfying and rewarding. What stops humans from gaining this high level of well-being is that many of us don't know how to get a job. Just the word *résumé* strikes fear in our hearts. Most of us can't pronounce the word, let alone know what it means. Have you ever heard anyone talk about "I got to do a résumé" instead of a "re-su-me" in this module. Not only will I show you how to prepare a résumé, I will show that it is not always important to have one.

Suppose someone told you, "I want you to work for nothing." You would probably think that person is crazy without realizing that this is an easy way to get a job. Imagine you put on your finest threads and had the greatest résumé and cover letter in the world and the interviewer just looked at you and said, "Sorry, John, we like your résumé, and you look good and all that, but you don't have any experience, and we are looking for someone with experience."

What would you do? Like most of us, you would stick your tail between your legs and leave. Wrong! Wrong! Wrong! This is just the opening you need. The first thing that should come out of your mouth is, "Yes, I understand, sir, but to gain this experience that I am missing, I am willing to work for your company for nothing. Not only will I work for nothing, I will work for as long as you want me to, doing whatever you want me to do. And if at any time you are not satisfied with my work, you can fire me."

I'll bet the interviewer drops his pen. Not only that, you might end up getting the job. He would be a fool if he did not take you up on your proposal to work for nothing. I know tons of people who started just that way, working for nothing. Some examples of this type of work are internships for college students, volunteer work, or apprenticeships.

Working for nothing can be deadly because there is no guarantee that the company you are working for will eventually hire you, but the chances are good, especially if you are doing a good job. Besides, you are also gaining valuable experience that can prove to be very beneficial in the future. If this is the only way you have a shot at getting a job, then by all means take it. You don't have anything to lose but some time. You don't have any money anyway, so what is the difference?

Chances are, small companies that are just starting out will be willing to take a chance on this arrangement. Just let me say here that working for nothing is not my original idea, but it makes a lot of sense. I read this idea in a book. My wording, however, is original. In any event, I am alerting you that you may need to be creative to land that elusive job. The best motto for you to land a job, however, is to be prepared. This is the key to the whole thing. Knowledge is power. Under all circumstances, get as much as you can.

The key to getting to get a good job is education. Get as much as you can. Just because you did not finish high school does not mean that you should give up and go on welfare and use the excuse that "I can't get a job because I don't have a high school diploma." Get one. Start by trying in your spare time to take some courses to prepare yourself to take the GED. Don't get discouraged. Keep taking it until you pass it. If it is necessary for you to go back to school, by all means, go back to school. You are never too old to go back to school. A very good friend of mine got her bachelor's degree at fifty-five. She used to always remark that she was the oldest person in her graduating class. She became a housing manager and had a very good career. She was once on welfare.

Most people don't know that there is a definite advantage to being poor. Everything is practically free, including an education. You can get free tuition, tap, Beog, and a host of other things. The poorer you are, the more financial aid you can get.

Unfortunately some of us, especially black Americans, don't realize that being poor has tremendous advantages. You see, when you are poor, education is practically free because financial aid is based on the principle of need. The poorer you are, the greater your chances of getting full financial aid, money you do not have to pay back, unlike student loans. It is even more demoralizing that we don't take advantage of this quirk by going to school as much as possible. If you are poor with all the financial aid available, you can practically get a PhD for nothing. In fact, you could practically go to school forever.

Pledge now to go back to school and apply for every conceivable financial aid that you can get because the chances are good that if you are poor, you will be able to get maximum financial aid and go to school forever. Families that make a decent salary have to pay for everything or get loans that must be paid back.

Look at me, for example. Because I make a decent salary, I have to pay for everything. My daughter who graduated from college got no help, but if I had little or no income, she could practically have gone go to college for nothing. Don't let the establishment or the government fill you full of drugs and alcohol and keep you on welfare because white America does not want blacks to gain the greatest gift of all, which is the gift of knowledge because knowledge is power and white America does not want blacks to have power. White America wants to keep you on welfare and drugs and in jail. Don't let them do this. You must take advantage of the system and get all of the education that you can and get off welfare.

Don't worry about getting a job because if you get a good education, the jobs will come to you. Besides if you can't get a job, you can always open your own business. In another one of my modules, I will teach you how to open your own business. In another one, I will teach you how to get off welfare because welfare is the ruination of our society. Welfare takes away your aspiration, that is, I mean your desire to do something.

Another gimmick that the system uses is the so-called special education classes whenever a child is not learning up to the establishment's standards. They tell you that your child has a learning disability, and they stick that child in some type of special education class. Learning is gaining knowledge, and all of us have the ability to gain knowledge as well as anyone if we are given a chance. Don't let someone else think for you. Remember, knowledge is power. Get all you can.

Now that we have talked about education, which is the first key step in getting a job, let us now focus our attention on the second key step, which is preparation. By now, I'm hoping that you have a PhD from Harvard or Yale or at least a bachelor's from some college or university. Nowadays an associate degree and a high school diploma are like the bare essentials, but by all means, I am not implying that you should not at least get one of those because someone who did not finish high school has a very little chance of getting a job. If they are fortunate enough to get one, they are making $200 per week. That person is even better than someone standing on the corner drinking forty ounces pretending to be a rap star or, worse yet, becoming a drug dealer, crack head, or a thief. If you are not working, you are going to do something. You will become part of the statistic of those young people who are the hunks in jail or markers in the cemetery. "Here lie the ones who lived so fast and died so young." If you want to be one of those, then this module is not for you because you can't be helped and I don't have any sympathy for you because you are stupid. I am trying to reach out to the ones of us who still have some sense.

You have the education, so now is the time to prepare. You will need a résumé and maybe a nice cover letter to get you that all-important interview. But before all of this, you need to know what you want to do. You might have a degree in electrical engineering and now realize that you want to be a funeral home director to take care of those people who are standing on the corner waiting to die. Hopefully your degree is in something you want to do, but if it is not, then it is not the end of the world. You just have a more intriguing possibility. The best and most rewarding jobs are the ones you like.

For example, if you like to paint pictures, you might get a job in an art field, like a museum or a studio. If you like dealing with people, you might become a counselor or a social worker. If you like providing housing, you might become a housing manager. Maybe you will feel good knowing that you helped to solve some of the homeless problems. In any event, your degree dictates your field or endeavor, but don't just rely on that if you find that some other field will make you happy. You are better off going with a job that makes you happy, even more so than money, because if you are not happy, it is too hard to go to work.

You have to think about where you are going to look for a job. A lot of us don't know where to find jobs. A simple thing like thumbing through the yellow pages will give you endless possibilities. The yellow pages break down different types of business alphabetically. The blue pages pretty much do the same thing with local, state, and federal agencies. This can be a good starting source. The library is another one. In addition, there are tons of employment offices, job training centers, and of course the want ads of your local paper. All of the sources that are mentioned are related to private or governmental organizations that are primarily for profit.

What about the not-for-profit organizations, like churches, synagogues, charities, health-care facilities, political offices, and so on? These organizations need employees as well. In fact, almost every type of organization, both private, public, profit, nonprofit, civil service, military, and anything you can think of, is a possibility for a job. You don't have to look very hard. There are endless possibilities. The key is to be prepared, which starts with a good education.

Let us turn our attention to the preparation of a résumé, cover letter, and job interviews. Let us start by defining a résumé, cover letter, and a job interview. A résumé is a short account or summary of a person's career, education, and qualification prepared specifically for a job or position. Most résumés have three or more basic parts. There is a beginning in which you indicate your purpose or intent or a statement summarizing what you are seeking. For example, you might be looking for an exciting executive position in hotel management where your experience, education, and supervisory expertise will allow for continued growth and future advancement.

The second part involves convincing the prospective reader that your education and qualification will meet the specific requirements for the position you are seeking. In other words, you attempt to give a chronological breakdown of your outstanding accomplishments, positions you hold or held in the past, projects you have accomplished, books you have published, or any worthwhile endeavor that you have been involved in. In layperson's terms, you attempt to sell yourself and your background

The third part involves listing your educational backgrounds, degrees you hold, certificates, licenses, and specialized skills such as computers, steno, word processing, and so on. By all means, if you graduated in the top five of your class or college, mention it, especially if it is from some prestigious college or university. In this part of your résumé, you also want to sell yourself because the better your background, the better your chances of getting a job or at least an interview.

The above three parts are always included in a résumé, but if you belong to some type of special organization like the Peace Corps or perhaps have won some special award like the Nobel Peace Prize, then by all means mention it. Another part often used is a reference, which is usually indicated as "references will be furnished upon request." If you are going to use references, by all means mention famous people you might have worked for and include a reference letter. This is very impressive. You must remember that your résumé highlights who you are. If you are able to make yourself stand out from the crowd, you have a better chance of getting that job.

Résumés are becoming more and more sophisticated, so uniqueness might be the key to presenting yourself. For example, you might want to include a synopsis of what you expect to do in the future instead of what you have done in the past. Sometimes it is not "What have you done for me lately?" but "What can you do for me now and in the future?"

Now let us talk a little bit about a cover letter. A good letter brings attention and arouses interest to the reader. It is like the prologue to a good play. It introduces the person, gives a brief synopsis of their background, and offers positive projections, like how your involvement can be beneficial to the organization. In other words, it sells your résumé, which will follow. Remember, all of this is intended to sell yourself, and companies want to buy the very best, just like you want to buy the very best.

So it is indeed very important to make that first impression a good one because your goal is to get your résumé past the garbage can and into the hands of someone who can hopefully make a decision. Your aim is to always show that you are a Rolls-Royce and not a Chevy. A good cover letter can prove invaluable, and a lousy one will get your résumé thrown into the garbage can.

Once you have completed your résumé and cover letter, if you need samples, I can send you some for a modest fee. You should make as many quality copies as possible and send them to prospective employers, using the system I explained earlier. Hopefully you will get several responses and offers to come to that all-important interview. This is the opportunity you have been waiting for, so take advantage of it by preparing. Do your homework by trying to learn as much about the company as possible. Go to the library, do research, talk to people who work there, or take the secretary to lunch. Do whatever it takes, short of sleeping with the president's wife, to gain this knowledge. Become the president. Also immediately put in your personalized order for the *Wall Street Journal* so you can prominently display it on top of your briefcase at the interview.

When you know you are thoroughly prepared enough to step in and be the company president because you know as much about the company as they do, then think in terms of your wardrobe. You want to select your best and best-pressed conservative suit that you have with a nice, clean white shirt and power tie to match. By all means, you should shine your shoes and get a shave and haircut for the interview. This is definitely the time to throw away those baggy pants and big, heavy boots. To be perfectly honest, you want to look like them. They can more readily identify with you if you dress and talk like them. You will have a greater chance at getting a job.

Don't panic. The chances are good that the person doing the interview was once in the same situation. If you are prepared, you will feel confident, and it will show in your demeanor. Sit up straight, relax, and act naturally. Don't try to be something that you are not. If you are confident and well prepared, the chances are good that you will land the job or be called back for a second interview by someone who is in a position to make a decision.

Under all circumstances, tell the truth because it is much easier to tell the truth than it is to remember the lies you told. Don't get discouraged if you don't land that all-important job the first time around. Rome was not built in a day. Keep trying. Send out those résumés and continue to cultivate at least one lead at every company you go to. Don't be afraid to meet people. The person you meet might just be the person to get you in the door. It is always a good idea to send the company a letter thanking them for giving you an interview and offering to be of further assistance. Always remember that once you get in the door, hard work and honesty will take you to the top. Good luck!

How To Get Good Grades

A good education is perhaps a key ingredient for becoming successful in life. The better the education, the better your chances of succeeding. If you obtain a PhD from Yale versus a high school diploma from Spring Valley High School, you have a much better chance of becoming successful. The average child can obtain a PhD from Yale if that child learns how to get good grades at a very young age. Unfortunately, many people believe you have to be very smart or intelligent to obtain a PhD from Yale. This analogy is perhaps true, but it is also possible for the average person with average intelligence to get a PhD from Yale when you learn the correct techniques for getting good grades. It is not always based on intelligence. Learning the discipline for getting good grades is just as important as being very smart. In fact, if you continue to get good grades, you will become very smart even though you only have average intelligence.

The first technique is based on increasing your ability to read effectively. This will improve your skills in all school subjects from history to calculus and from any form of math and science. Just like building a house requires a foundation, reading effectively is the base for getting good grades. The problem with children, especially boys, is that they hate to read. Not only are they missing out on a whole new exciting world, they are hindering their chances of becoming successful. The key to learning is to be able to read effectively. And to do that is by learning how to comprehend what you have read. This can be accomplished when you know the meaning of the words you read and can relate those words to your everyday life.

A simple technique for doing this is to always carry a note pad or a small dictionary with you. When you are reading things like books, magazines, or newspapers and you come across a word that you don't know the meaning of, you can either look up the word in your dictionary or write the word down for future look-up. I know this technique is laborious, but it is very rewarding, and you will find that your vocabulary, conversations, and understanding will increase tenfold.

If you continue to use this technique, you will become so good at writing and understanding the written words that you will amaze yourself. If you take tests like standardized civil service exams, you will always do very well. Your problem-solving abilities and your ability to comprehend will be greatly improved. If you can ever master this technique, you are on your way to the top because all your grades will improve.

The second technique for getting good grades is to develop the discipline necessary. And this comes from studying effectively. You need to know how to study. In your room with the radio and/or TV blasting is the way that most of us study, but that is not the most effective way. The atmosphere for studying is peace and tranquility. The dormitory is normally not conducive for studying because of the many distractions. Other students will constantly interrupt you with their loud radios or visits to your room. It is very difficult to study under these circumstances.

As much as you dislike the library, this is perhaps the best place to study because it is supervised and monitors keep the noise level to a minimum. Not only is that true, all reference books, computers, and other resources are at your fingertips. In addition, you are surrounded by other students who are studying instead of those in the dormitory who are trying to get you to go out to party. Therefore, creating the proper atmosphere is the first method for learning how to study. The right atmosphere is the library and not your dormitory room.

The second step in learning how to study is time management. More difficult courses require a greater amount of time. You should concentrate on the more difficult courses first because if you run out of time, then you can use the smaller amount of time on the easier courses. It is also more difficult to get good grades in difficult courses like calculus, chemistry, and physics. Although these courses may be difficult to most people, they may not be difficult for you. Therefore, it is important for you to determine which courses are difficult for you and concentrate on those first. Deciding which courses to spend the greater amount of time in studying will help you with time management.

The third step in learning how to study is to know how to deal with course contents, for instance, seeing importance placed on classroom notes, following the written materials in the book, or understanding the solutions in the book or classroom. Learning this technique is the key to getting good grades. You can usually learn this based on the teacher by assessing the teachers or just asking them what should be emphasized.

In a very large classroom setting, it is very difficult to get individual attention, so it becomes important for you to learn how to work independently of the teacher, but to do this, you need to know what makes the teacher tick. Some teachers follow the course outline verbatim; others stray back and forth, inserting life situations into the materials. You need to know what type of teacher you are dealing with in order to master the course and get good grades.

Every teacher might be similar in their approach, but they also might be very different depending on the course being taught. Courses like history, sociology, and psychology are reading courses, and the teacher might strictly be a lecturer. Unfortunately, these courses may be very boring, and it becomes difficult to stay awake. So, you might have to read, work, and write independently of the teacher. Courses like science and math may be easier to follow because examples and problems are used to explain the course contents.

In any event, you need to know what type of teacher you are dealing with to help you develop your time management approach to studying. Under normal circumstances, you must look at studying as having at least a part-time job, for instance, twenty hours per week. If you do this every week, you are definitely on your way to a PhD from Yale.

Just like having a job, every now and then, you need a day off. All work and no play makes Jack a dull boy. It is therefore important for you to determine how to allocate your time for maximum results. The best approach is to leave your weekend open so you don't become a candidate for burnout. If you use this approach, you need to study four hours a day for five days, which translates to twenty hours per week. The difficulties with this approach are what are meant by developing the discipline for studying.

Most people refuse to develop the necessary discipline for studying, and as result, they fail to get good grades. If you stop to think about it, four hours per day appears to be a lot, but if you break up those four hours into intervals, you will find that it can be done easily. For example, Monday, Wednesday, and Friday are maybe your heavy days for classes, but even during those days you may have one to three hours between classes, and this would be the perfect time to spend quality time in the library between classes. The afternoon classes are usually over by 6:00 p.m., but you probably don't go to bed until 11:00 p.m. So that gives you five hours right there.

Before we go any further, let us examine a few techniques for effective studying. Note taking is perhaps the most common method for recording information given in class. The thing, however, with note taking is that we cannot record everything the teacher said, or in our haste to record everything that was said, we miss a lot of important points. It therefore becomes absolutely necessary to review and confirm your notes to information in the book or the syllabus to ensure your chance for success. In situations when problems are used as a method for teaching, it is important to go over the problems after you leave the classroom to make sure you understand what was done. You should also create several new problems with different variations to reinforce your capabilities.

Another technique for studying is to create exams at various intervals in the chapter based on your experiences with the teacher on how they might arrange an exam. When you read, it is always a good idea to highlight important information and make written notes to yourself for memorization and concentration. It seems that you can remember things much better if you write down the information. I am sure that you can think of other techniques for effective studying, but as always, the key to doing anything well is preparation. You must constantly prepare yourself for success.

The best method for studying for an exam is not staying up all night, or "burning the midnight oil." Not only will you be tired and sleepy, you will forget everything you studied once you fall asleep because the brain and body are tired and stressed out.

The best method for studying is not to wait until the last minute, but if you must, you should go to bed really early and arise really early in the morning to study. You will find that your mind and body are more refreshed because they are well rested and you will be able to retain much more information using this method. Now that we have learned how to study, we can proceed to the final method for getting good grades, how to become a good test-taker.

Exams have a profound effect on every aspect of our lives. We take an IQ exam to determine how intelligent we are. We take PSAT and SAT exams to determine what schools we can go to. We take doctors' exams to determine how well we are. We take civil service exams to get jobs and promotions and so on. It seems every day we are taking some kind of an exam.

Nothing is truer then when it comes to school: pop quizzes, midterms, and finals are the norm. Doing well on exams determines almost everything we do in life. If you cannot pass the bar exam, you can't become a lawyer. If you don't pass the CPA exam, you can't become a certified public accountant. When it comes to school, if you can't pass the exams, you don't graduate. So it behooves you to learn how to become a good test-taker unless you want to become a professional student.

There are generally two types of exams that you encounter in school and the job environment: essays and multiple choices. Completion and matching exams are variations of these two types. If you are dealing with math and science courses, problem-solving exams are more suitable. Let us examine the multiple-choice type, which is the most common.

On the multiple-choice exam, there are two key ingredients that you must be familiar with in addition to knowing how to read and interpret the question. The first technique normally used is key words or phrases, such as the best or least method for accomplishing a problem, the highest or lowest value for the equation, or the most or least desirable course of action to follow. In these types of questions, the first answer you calculate is not always the correct answer because it very well might be an answer, but it is not the best or least answer. For example, if you were a rent collector and visited an apartment to collect rents and the tenant told you "I don't have the money," what is the best course of action for you to follow?

A. Curse the tenant and leave.
B. Advise the tenant that you will pay the rent for her for today only.
C. Slap the tenant in the face and demand the rent.
D. Ask the tenant when she will be able to pay.
E. None of the above

If you examine the answers, you can see that every answer is a course of action to follow, but the best course of action to follow would be answer D. Ask the tenant when she will be able to pay. In this same question, if you were asked to determine the least course of action to follow, your answer would be a toss-up between cursing the tenant and leaving or slapping the tenant in the face and demanding the rent. Both of these actions are not desirable, but slapping the tenant in the face would be the least desirable.

The second technique often used in multiple-choice type questions is the process of elimination. Generally you can eliminate two of the answers right away. In the example cited above, cursing and slapping the tenant could be eliminated right away because it is not very professional or sane to do either one. Once you have done this, you are usually left with two good choices.

In this same example, the two good choices might have been to ask the tenant when she will be able to pay or none of the above. When you examine these two good choices, asking the tenant when she will be able to pay shows consideration and concern for her situation. None of the above could have been selected because you could have said to the tenant, "Well, I am sorry, but I will be forced to pursue legal action to collect the rent."

This might be fine except that the question asked "Which is the best course of action to follow?" which implies that some course of action should be taken, and telling the tenant "I will be forced to pursue legal action" was not one of the choices. Oftentimes a good idea is to read the answers before you read the question. Usually if you do this, the two stupid answers can be eliminated right away.

Even if you don't know the answer once you eliminate the two obviously wrong answers, you have a fifty-fifty chance of getting the correct answer. In multiple-choice type questions, the remaining two answers are very close to being the correct answer. The key thing is to examine the question very carefully to see if there are any key words or phrases that will give you a clue to the best or correct answer.

Essay exams are much more difficult than multiple-choice exams. In essay exams, you must know the subject matter extremely well to write effectively. The teacher can immediately tell if you are bullshitting. Not only must you deal with the subject matter, you must also deal with the correct grammar. An essay consists of three basic parts: an introduction, a body, and a conclusion.

Since an essay can be somewhat subjective, it is overly important to determine what is expected before you can even begin to write the introduction. The subject matter must be dissected, analyzed, and scrutinized to determine the essential points that the examiner is looking to get from the writer. The best way to do this is to reverse the role of the examiner and the writer. In other words, you become the teacher, and then you decide what the teacher wants you to bring out in the essay.

Once you have done this, you are ready to begin brainstorming to prepare an outline. In brainstorming, you make a list of everything that comes to mind regarding the subject matter. This is equivalent to gathering information to solve a problem. After you have done this, you are ready to review and analyze the information to determine how best to utilize it. This technique should help you to prepare an outline to begin your essay. The outline is like a road map to keep you from drifting or going off on a tangent. It is a very important tool to use in writing essays because it keeps you organized, precise, and concise. So you are now ready to start the introduction.

The introduction begins with the purpose, or intent, of the essay. It highlights what is to be accomplished. It is very much like introducing a speaker. It gives a brief description of the speaker's background and how they fit into the big picture. The main focus of the introduction is to inform and explain what is to be expected. Depending on the subject matter, it can be quite long or just a few short paragraphs. Once you complete the introduction, you are ready to focus on the meat and potatoes of the easy. The body is where you do this.

The body depicts the full essence of your essay. It is a detailed exposition of factual information to support your hypothesis, expounding on sources, references, methods, procedures, experiments, and other data to support your findings. The body is usually much longer and much more detailed than the introduction. It carries the burden of proof using inductive and deductive reasoning. By this, I mean you begin with a central theme and add to or subtract factual inferences to arrive at a conclusion. A simple example would be if a is equal to b and b is equal to c then a must also be equal to c. This is known as the theory of equality. The body is therefore comprehensive and intended to establish the facts to support your findings.

The third part of the essay is the summary, or conclusion. It would be considered the wrap-up to your essay. It allows you the opportunity to reinforce your objectives to enlighten your reader on how to benefit from your findings and monitor and follow up on the things that you have learned or tried to express.

In summary, getting good grades involve a three-prong approach. The first thing is to become an effective reader. Once you have done that, you must develop the discipline necessary to get good grades, and that can only come from studying. It does not matter how smart you are. You must use some type of preparation to achieve greatness. The third thing involves becoming an excellent test taker using some of the techniques described in this module. If you try hard enough, there is nothing that can stop you from doing well in life.

How to Get Off Welfare

When you talk about getting off welfare, you must understand that many people on welfare don't want to get off it. These are the people whom I call the wannabes. They are on welfare because they want to be on it. Generally they are too lazy and stupid to believe that welfare deprives them of self-worth. They have no value system.

They are content at being the wards of society, barely literate and able to carry on a decent conversation. Every other word out of their mouth is "mother fucker this" and "mother fucker that." Most people of this type are too stupid to realize that the key to the whole universe is knowledge, which brings power, and power brings money and success.

The second group of people on welfare is the have-to-bees. They are on welfare because they have to be on it. They are on welfare because they might be old and can't work, or they might be slightly retarded or deficient in some capacity.

For example, a person might have worked all of their life, and suddenly the company goes bankrupt. The person is fifty-five years old—too young to collect Social Security and too old to get another decent job due to limited knowledge, education, or skills. Someone like this might be forced to go on welfare. The chances are the have-to-bees dread being on welfare because welfare is like a stigma, signifying they are worthless. Folks like these are on welfare because they have to be on it.

So the question becomes: how do we get off welfare? Certainly not the way the government proposed for you by creating some meager-paying job like sweeping the streets and cleaning the parks. In reality, the government doesn't want you to get off welfare. What would they do with all the money that the welfare system creates? They tell you that they want you to get off welfare to save face, when in reality, the establishment wants a lot of people to stay poor with little or no education because they can continue to control you by giving you a meager check every fifteen days. They in turn continue to collect millions.

Welfare is the very worst that is wrong with society because it breeds dependence instead of independence. When you don't have to work for your money to earn a living, you begin to rationalize and makes excuses. You begin to say, "Why should I work when I can stay in bed until twelve thirty when the *Young and Restless* (or some other stupid soap opera or talk show) comes on?" You begin to make excuses that hinder your desire to sharpen your mind through knowledge. An idle mind is the devil's workshop.

Crime, drugs, alcoholism, prostitution, and all other deviant social disorders are more prevalent among welfare families because the little money that is given to them is not enough to live on. So to get more money, they resort to having more babies, selling their minds and bodies, committing more crimes, and so on.

People on welfare as well as the government don't understand that the way to get off welfare is not about stupid workforce jobs that the government espouses. They want you to work in some meaningless jobs that they themselves would not do. The way to get off welfare is not about these stupid jobs. So, the question becomes: Just how do we get off welfare?

People on welfare as well as government don't understand that the way to get off welfare is not through meaningless jobs but the education of your minds. To get off welfare is through the education of the mind, body, and spirit. People must be made to believe that their lives have a purpose, a meaning, and a spirit. This can only be done through education. Forget about the meager jobs. Schools must be created.

Training centers must be created with the goal of producing skilled labor such as electricians, plumbers, mechanics, computer technicians, internet workers, and so on. People must be made to believe that if they get a good education, there will be good jobs for them, not careers like sweeping the streets and cleaning the parks.

In fact, people on welfare must be encouraged to go back to school. They should be told that if they do not return to school, they will be removed from welfare, much more so than missing a face-to-face interview or working at some meaningless job to receive their checks. The ultimate threat for removal from welfare should be the threat of not attending school, which would lead to the closing of their welfare case. Knowledge is power, and knowledge through education is the key for getting off welfare. The government should propose that every welfare family must have at least a high school diploma to remain on welfare. This alone will make a much better society.

The late John F. Kennedy once said, "Ask not what your country can do for you, but ask what you can do for your country." What you can do for your country as poor welfare families or any other family is to take advantage of the welfare system through the use of an education. If you are poor and on welfare, education is free. People on welfare have the greatest gift in the world by being able to get an education for nothing. The only requirement is to maintain good grades. The system is set up so that financial aid is based on the need allowance. Scholarships, grants, and most types of financial aid are generally based on need, and people on welfare are often poor enough to get the entire spectrum of financial aid.

In essence, families on welfare can get all the financial aid that is needed to allow them to go to college for practically nothing. This is the key for getting off welfare, by taking advantage of a system that allows you to obtain a college education for free. This is a very simple plan that can easily be executed. The key, however, is to refocus your mind away from things that encourage dependence. Talk shows, soap operas, and other stupid TV shows must be cast aside. In their place, you must substitute a plan of action to return to school. This is the hardest part of refocusing your mind.

Every single person who is unable to read and write is ashamed to let it be known. As a result, these folks become functional illiterates. Unless we as a people can get beyond this shame, we will always be the wards of society. You cannot expect to get very far if you cannot read and write. The system is set up so that at any interval on the educational scale, there is a starting point for every single person, whether you need to start at the beginning by learning to read and write or whether you need to get your high school diploma or college degree.

The problem is that you must start at some point. The *Young and the Restless*, *Judge Judy*, *Judge Mathis*, and other meaningless TV shows will not help you. You must cast away your shame and go back to school, no matter what the circumstances are. An education is the first step in establishing self-worth. With self-worth, you will want to get off welfare.

The second step to getting off welfare is to refocus the spirit. Any form of organized religion will help you to do this. It does not matter whether you are Jewish or Gentile, Catholic or Protestant, Methodist or Baptist, Buddhist or Hindu, Muslim or Chinese, and so on. All religions work on the spirit and/or the mind. Every person is a sinner through the flesh, but the mind should be the epitome of the spirit where belief is based on faith that our superior will deliver us.

The third step to getting off welfare is to refine the body. A good-looking body is the essence of high self-esteem. When you look and feel good, your mind tends to change from a negative to a positive. You can accomplish this by eating sensibly and walking a lot more than riding.

Therefore, we can summarize how to get off welfare into three steps:

1. Return to school and get all the education that is possible.
2. Refocus your spirit by returning to some type of religious institution.
3. Refine your body through proper diet and exercise.

If you can do these three simple steps, you will cease to be a ward of society dependent upon a welfare check every fifteen days. These three steps will give you high self-worth and enhance your ability to get off welfare and gain a good job. If you cannot find a good job, you will have enough self-esteem to create your own job by opening up some type of business. Every business does not require a lot of money. In fact, most service businesses require little or no cash. Use your natural talent to start your own business. Start your business doing something that you do best, and someone will be willing to pay you to do that service for them.

The question becomes: what to do if all of these welfare families return to school? Most of these families receive aid to dependent children. What will happen to all of these children, and who will care for them? Well, there is a simple solution to this problem. These children can attend daycare centers while their mothers and fathers return to school. The families receiving home relief can be used to help run the daycare centers. Many more daycare centers will be needed, which will require new construction, new teachers, and so on.

This large influx of children into the daycare industry will create new jobs through additional staffing and construction. As families who return to school graduate and need jobs, there will already be a ready supply for them in the daycare industry. As families continue to pursue an education, more and more families will get off welfare and become productive members of society. Every industry will benefit from this new pool of well-trained members of society.

Many of these families, however, have serious social problems. How will this problem be addressed? Screening centers can be used to eliminate these social problems after a complete investigation into the background of the workers who will become employed in the daycare centers. Hardened criminals, child molesters, and other deviant social disorders can be weeded out using available resources such as the Department of Social Services. The Department of Social Services, using available resources and new funds created from the savings from families getting off welfare, can take a proactive role in this endeavor.

As this process unfolds, welfare will become less of a stigma, and welfare families will begin to believe that their lives have meaning and a purpose. In addition, this endeavor will better serve society. This process can become a spiraling effect as more and more people become educated, they will be able to find rewarding and well-paying good jobs so there will be no need for welfare. The daycare centers would become self-sustaining because the monies that will be saved can be used to fund them. This process will create a more diverse society that will enhance a better quality of life for all of us. So in summary, getting off welfare involves getting a good education for the mind, body, and spirit, and everything else will fall into place.

How to Get Rid of Crime

When you think about how to get rid of crime, you must look at some of the root causes of crime before you can even think in terms of how to get rid of it. Let us examine some of the causes of crime, such as greed, poverty, drugs, lack of education, welfare, mental illness, rage, hatred, and a host of other mental and social disorders. If you get rid of these things, you remove crime. Just how to go about this perhaps is on the agenda of every politician in the country with little success.

Crime continues to be a tremendous burden on all aspects of life, from replacing your child's stolen bike to your stolen car. How to get rid of crime can be debated over and over to building more jails, increasing the police force, getting families off welfare, creating more drug centers, and so on. None of these things appear to help because crime continues to be just as evident as life and death.

When we think of how to get rid of crime, we are actually thinking in terms of how to reduce it. The goal is to reduce the effect of crime on our everyday life. This can be done in a series of steps centered around the causes of crime. In this module, I will attempt to address how to get rid of crime through an examination of a series of steps. The opinions expressed herein are the opinions of this writer as seen from his experiences.

To get rid of crime, you need to examine different facets of crime, such as crime involving drugs, domestic violence, love and hatred, rage

101

and vengeance, and white- and blue-collar crime such as bank and stock frauds, money laundering, petty theft, car robbery, and so on. When you look at each of these different facets of crime, there are three basic themes. They are generally centered among poverty, greed, or mental illness due to a lack of education or a serious social disorder.

Greed is perhaps the greatest cause of white-collar crimes like bank or stock fraud, embezzlement, money laundering, and political corruption. Unfortunately to become successful you must have a sense of greed. If you are not greedy, it is difficult to have the resolve to become successful in business. Greed stems from the drive to be the best, and it is difficult to be the best saying, "I don't want it all! I only want a little bit."

The greedy person wants the championship ring. He wants it all. Capitalism is built on this principle although many people will not admit it, the principle of pure competition is the essence of capitalism, and it is built on the principle of greed. When someone examines a greedy person, they are looking at a selfish person who thrives to gain the best of everything. You cannot be the very best unless you believe "I can do this better than anyone else" and be willing and able to prove it repeatedly.

Athletes are a good example. You must be greedy and hungry to win the ultimate goal, the goal of the champion. If you are working around the specter of money and the influences of money such as bankers, stockbrokers, politicians, lobbyists, corporation presidents, and so on, it is easy to understand how you could become greedy. The more money you have, the more power and influence you have, and you would not be very smart if you did not want it all. Hence the principle of greed comes into play. If you get a chance to get more and more money without being convicted of a crime, there is a good chance that you would take it. Money is far ahead of whatever is in second place.

Now that we have examined a little bit of what is meant about being greedy, we can access how to cure or temper this character or possibly this flaw in humankind. Let me start by saying that greed is good for humankind, but only under controlled conditions. This principle I define as "control greed," the willingness to be greedy, but not at the expense of others, and the willingness to be greedy, but not willing to help or elevate others. In other words, it is okay to be greedy, but it is not okay to be selfish and greedy. Although I don't know LeBron James, he impressed me as someone who exhibits control greed. He thrives to be the best, but he is willing to sacrifice his efforts so others can achieve greatness as well.

I am not saying that white-collar crime involves only selfish, greedy despots who manipulate the system at the expense of others to gain the advantage of money because of its power and influence. There are other reasons for white-collar crime such as extreme medical problems. There are people who are involved in the specter of money who are faced with serious medical problems that have consumed all of their savings, and they commit white-collar crime due to desperation and love for the sufferer. In essence, these folks are definitely not acting out of greed. Their crime is a crime of passion or love and must be dealt with in a totally different manner.

The overriding reason for white-collar crime in my opinion, however, is based on greed. The way to reduce white-collar crime is for every company or organization to offer their employees courses in the causes and effects of white-collar crime and crime in general and how it impacts on the life of the company, public, and employees it serves.

In addition, employee assistance programs should have confidential counselors to address this problem instead of investing millions of dollars in surveillance equipment to catch employees committing some type of crime. To reduce crime, you must address what is causing crime instead of doing something after the person has been caught.

Now that we have examined white-collar crime, let us examine blue-collar crime, which I define as the crime of poverty. As I said before, there are three basic themes centered throughout crime, one of which is greed and the other being poverty and mental illness due to a lack of education or deviant social behavior. Although blue-collar crime implies crime committed by working people, poverty in some form, whether it be mild or extreme, is the root cause of this type of crime. I know it is difficult to associate working people with poverty, but when you stop to think about it, it is not difficult at all.

The majority of blue-collar workers barely make more than the minimum wage established by the government. The minimum wage is the line of poverty. If you are making something near the minimum wage, you are living in poverty. Unfortunately your income determines everything about you. It determines where you live, where you eat, and where you make love. If you are making the minimum wage, it is almost impossible for you not to be living in the ghetto or not to eat at McDonalds. Certainly you won't be living in the Hamptons and making love in the Plaza Hotel.

The bulk of crime committed by working families occur among this group of workers. Why? Well, the simple truth is that they don't have enough money to live on. They can exist in meager surroundings, punctuated by crime and drugs and a liquor store on every corner. But are they living? The fact is, they are existing and cannot wait for the opportunity to steal from the employer that provides a job for them. They know that 90 percent of the wealth in the world and certainly in America is owned by 10 percent of the population. They know that their employer is one of the 1 0 percent, and chances are, they will not become one of the 10 percent.

Poverty is perhaps the greatest cause of crime in this country. It creates almost every other type of social deviant behavior, from drug abuse to alcoholism to prostitution. Poverty comes from two sources, one from working at very low wages and the other from welfare and other nonworking forms of income like Disability and Social Security. These people are forced to exist, and unfortunately the worse their conditions are, the more they resort to crime to either soothe their misery or supplement their income. There are many people with barely enough money to live on. They are forced to become the wards of society dependent upon the government, families, and friends. It is sad to say that ghettoes exist because of poverty, and crime emanates from poverty because a hungry dog will find a way to eat.

There are two ways to get food when you don't have enough to feed and clothe your family, either from begging or stealing. You get tired of begging, so you steal and sell drugs. Building more prisons and creating more drug centers will not help to get rid of crime. A hundred million jails and treatment centers will not get rid of crime. Eliminating poverty, however, will go a long way toward eliminating crime because it addresses one of the root causes of crime, which is poverty. This can be helped by a substantial increase in the minimum wage law so the minimum wage is at least $20 per hour for any and every type of job.

Mental illness to include a lack of education and mental instability are the other major contributors to crime. If you can somehow encourage everyone to get a good education and find a way to get everyone to achieve this goal, then crime would be substantially reduced. I remember reading an article that stated the majority of people in prisons are high school dropouts, barely illiterate enough to carry on a decent conversation without cursing every other word. Why is this true?

It is apparently true because there is a direct correlation between crime and education. It is my belief that if you are uneducated, it is much easier for you to be influenced to go commit a crime to feel important or to placate your requester. I believe that your ability to reason between right and wrong is questionable at the lower levels of the educational spectrum.

Mental instability encompasses a whole range of crime-causing agents. Domestic violence as well as crimes of passion, rage and hatred, and racism and prejudice are some of the crimes that readily come to mind. And these crimes of emotion are much more prevalent than we care to think. I would imagine if you were able to get a correct assessment of every family, you would find that a crime of emotion is committed every day. The newspapers, radio, TV, and other media sources are full of stories illustrating this fact. Husbands are killing their wives and children before killing themselves. Day traders are walking into offices and killing coworkers. Students are walking into schools and killing their classmates. Terrorists are blowing up buildings and airplanes. Mothers are having babies and leaving them in trash cans. People are committing suicide, and religious fanatics are committing all sort of atrocities.

Are the people committing these crimes mentally stable? Absolutely not, but what can be done to eliminate this antisocial behavior. How do you stop a terrorist from being a terrorist? How do you stop a man from beating the crap out of his wife? How do you stop mothers and fathers from killing their babies? How do you stop the mob from killing each other? How do you stop the fighting in the Middle East, Syria, and Africa?

The only way to stop crime of this and any nature is through a total spiritual revolution where every person must forget the past in connection to who they are and concentrate on the present and future to find the commonality among people instead of the differences. They must be made to concentrate on what they are instead of who they are. Guns, other weapons, and all methods of mass destruction, including bombs and nuclear weapons, must be eliminated throughout the world. A oneness of spirit of the mind must be put into place to show every person on the face of the earth that they are one people with one goal, the purity of the heart, mind, and body.

I believe that the time is fast approaching where humankind will destroy itself. The path of violence escalating throughout the world will be the catalyst for this destruction unless we decide how to live in peace. This can only be done when the world believes that we are all the same. No human is better than his fellow human. When that belief becomes evident, there will be no need for extreme poverty and wealth in the world. Everybody would have as much as they need, and no one human would be able to own all the wealth while millions of their fellow humans own nothing.

Crime as it exists in today's society will never be eliminated, but we as a people can go far to reduce it by renewing our faith in God Almighty while searching for the commonality among all people with the determination that we are all the same. No man or woman is better than another.

How to Help Stop Racism

Racism is the fundamental belief that one set of people is better than another. The Germans during Hitler's days believed they were the master race. The white American race believes they are better than the black American race or vice versa. In actuality, racism is common throughout the world. Many wars and battles have been fought—and continue to be fought—because of this belief, although these struggles are not described as racism. It really means the same thing. They are due to religious, political, or ideological reasons, but in reality, one set of people believes that their way of life is better than another.

Racism is not only prevalent among the races. It is prevalent among the same races. Look at the American white race, for example. Different people within the white race believe they are better than other white people within the same race. The same is true for blacks, Chinese, Russians, and so on. There is nothing fundamentally wrong with being racist. In fact, being a racist is healthy. It helps to build high self-esteem. The problem comes into existence when one race of people attempts to impose their will on another set using force or other methods of coercion, genocide, and mistreatments.

The ultimate form of extreme racism is slavery, involuntary servitude, or clandestine operators like the Ku Klux Klan. You see, the problem with racism is that many racists are willing to act on their differences with other races of people. They are willing to deprive a person of equality in housing, education, civil rights, pursuit of happiness, or any other fundamental right that each person is entitled to. Superiority comes from deprivation. If one race of people is deprived of certain aspects of life over a long enough period of time, the race doing the depriving will become superior. It does not matter whether you are black, white, green, or purple. If you are being deprived, you will become inferior over a period of time. If a white kid in Mobile, Alabama, did not have an opportunity to go to school and a black kid in the same town had an opportunity to go to Harvard, then it appears quite likely that the white kid would be inferior to the black kid.

What I am trying to say is that superiority and inferiority between races are based on opportunity and the choices that one person makes compared to another. I believe that if you took normal newborn babies from each race and placed them in the same controlled environment with the exact same stimuli, they would become adults who would be so similar that nobody would be able to distinguish any differences.

The way to stop racism is based on the principles of deprivation and opportunity through a spiritual revelation. As a people, we must refocus our beliefs. We must forget about who we are and focus on who we can become. We must forget about the past because in actuality we do not know what happened then. You only know what has happened in your own lifetime. The things that have caused all the problems in the world have been based on what people believe that they were in the past. The Jews believe they are the chosen people. The Muslims believe they are the descendants of the last great prophet. Blacks believe they are the original man.

Fortunately or unfortunately, nobody knows. We can only speculate on what has happened in the past beyond our own life based on what we have read, heard from someone older than we are, or seen in movies or TV. We look at people all over the world and surmise that we all belong to the same race, that is, the human race. Our hair texture, eyes, and skin pigmentation may be different, but we are all humans and therefore must surmise that we all evolved the exact same way from a man and a woman.

From that perspective, we are exactly the same. There are many types of plants and animals, but there is only one type of human, either a man or a woman, both with the ability to walk upright and to speak under normal circumstances. The other thing about humans is that all of them have an ability to think and to reason under normal circumstances.

But even beyond that, there is a spiritual quality among all humans. I don't care how rudimentary that quality may be. It exists. That spiritual quality should be the binding force between races. The body is made of flesh, but the spiritual quality of humankind is from inside, that is, the mind.

To stop racism, we must refocus our mind. We must begin to truly believe that God created every man, woman, and child in His own image, which is the image of perfection. Now think about this. If God is perfect, why He would create inequality among man? We must believe that all men are created equal with certain unalienable rights. Among them are life, liberty, and the pursuit of happiness. The founders of the Constitution apparently believed this, but circumstances in society caused them to go astray just as circumstances continue to do so even until today.

The spiritual quality of humankind must be brought back into society. There is nothing wrong with prayers in school. There is nothing wrong with encouraging kids to create spiritual music instead of rap music, creating positive images of women instead of degradation, and promoting peace and love instead of violence. You see, if a spiritual quality is reinforced among the races, there would be a lesser chance of deprivation and a greater chance of opportunity. There would be a lesser chance of an abundance of poor, starving people all over the world and a few rich people sucking the blood from these poor people.

If a spiritual quality is reinforced in the world, there would be a society that looks at the contents of a person's character instead of the color of his skin and the contents of their pocketbook. Little children being starved of the basic necessities in life like food and clothing would be nonexistent. There would be no stealing and no hatred because "you don't look the same as I do" or "you don't wear the same clothes I do."

True opportunities would exist for everyone, and racism would truly become extinct.

How this utopia can be created should be our goal. The government must be at the forefront. The separation of the church and state must be removed. In its place, the thinking should be church first followed by the state or at least a combination of church and state. Unfortunately religion is the greatest thing that divides us. Jews are against Gentiles. Protestants are against Catholics. Muslims are against Christians. Buddhists are against Hindus. We must refocus that we are one and the same. We are neither Jew nor Gentile, neither Catholic nor Protestant, neither Buddhist nor Hindu, neither Christian nor Muslim, and so on. We are one and the same.

Our religion is the human religion. The thing that binds us should be our spirits, and we should look for the things that are common instead of the qualities that are different. This is the only way that racism and all worldly problems like fighting, quarrelling, genocide, murder, and other atrocities can be eliminated.

How to Start a Business

Necessity is sometimes the mother of invention. Often when people become unemployed, they are forced to find other means of supporting themselves and their families. Some people turn to crime, but more and more people should be turning to opening their own business. In this module, we will attempt to establish how to start a business from beginning to end, knowing that business is not an exact science and anything can happen.

Business can best be defined in simple terms as buying and selling goods and services. For example, clothing stores buy and sell clothing. A manufacturing company makes a particular item and sells it to a distributor, wholesaler, retailer, and so on. An accountant performs a service by preparing financial reports, conducting an audit, preparing budgets, and receiving payments for his or her services. The barber does the same.

To start a business, usually an idea is first considered. Research is done to see if this idea is unique; how it can be accomplished; how much it is going to cost to produce, market, and sell; whom the idea will be sold to; and how much you will make as a profit. Sometimes a business is also started from a business that is already in existence (e.g., you might work as an accountant for a large accounting firm and decide to strike out on your own. This can be done in any business.

For example, you are a painter working for the housing authority and decide to open your own painting firm. Even if you decide not to open the business yourself, you and a buddy could open it. If you are dealing with your idea and it is unique, you might want to sell licensing contracts. For example, when I was a kid, I had an idea for a windshield wiper on the back window of a car. Suppose I had that idea licensed and sold it to General Motors and they agreed to pay me a one-dollar royalty on every windshield wiper that was sold. Imagine the possibilities.

Suppose I had another idea about placing a pop-up razor on an electric shaver that would allow people to trim their mustaches and beards. Or think about toys for a minute. Suppose you created the Cabbage Patch doll, Mickey Mouse, GI Joe, and so on. Think of household appliances. What if you created the blender? In other words, if you come up with a unique idea, get it licensed, and receive a 5 percent royalty on each item that is sold, you could become rich very easily. Hello, Bill Gates.

Opening a business is the same. Unique ideas make millionaires. So when you lose your good-paying job after putting in twenty years, your life is not over. This might be the necessity that will spurn invention. Many of the things you have learned in the past years can be used to start your own business. Sometimes you don't need a lot of money to do so.

You could start tons of businesses with little or no money. Look at hairdressers or barbers, manicurists, hot dog vendors, babysitting or grocery shopping services, car washers, snow removers, grass cutters, tax preparers, painters, interior decorators, and all types of service-oriented businesses. Unfortunately prostitutes can fall into this category as well.

One of my friends started a house-cleaning business with his wife, and almost immediately, they were cleaning office buildings, supermarkets, banks, and so on. Needless to say, they are well off right now. They started with no money, just two people willing to work hard for themselves. There is a big difference between working hard for yourself and working hard for someone else. They drive BMWs, have a fleet of vans, live in a huge house, and have all the other trappings of being rich. Another friend of mine started a business installing ceiling fans, washing machines, water heaters, and cable TV. He learned these things by living in a house where he did those things because he could not pay someone else to do it. He is also doing very well with seven stores, maybe even one near you.

Needless to say, the easiest and least expensive business to open is a service. It is just a matter of thinking about something that you do and selling your services, usually by word of mouth and some clever, inexpensive advertising. Some of us become discouraged because we don't know how to get the paperwork completed that is required to open a business. We don't realize that a trip to the local library can give us more than enough information on how to open a business, how to complete the paperwork, and anything else we want to know. The truth is that most of us are very lazy and would rather pay someone to do it for us. Hello, lawyers.

Three types of businesses can be formed: a sole proprietorship, a partnership, or a corporation. Very recently a limited liability company has come into existence. This holds true whether we are talking about a service or a domestic business where a product is made and sold. Generally a business is licensed in the state where you live, but for tax reasons, you might license your business in a different state. This is sometimes referred to as a foreign business.

No matter what your preference is, the paperwork for each can usually be obtained from a local stationery store that carries Blumberg forms, named for the man who invented them. Now the big question becomes, Which form of a business should you open?

The easiest and least expensive business to open is the sole proprietorship. These businesses are usually referred to as one-owner businesses, for example, local grocery stores, newspaper shops, dry cleaning stores, shoe repair shops, barber shops, hairdressers, and so forth. In fact, most of the small companies in the United States are sole proprietorships. Because they are the least expensive, they carry the greatest tax liability. Taxes are based on the earnings of the individual owner, and the individual owner can be sued, and their personal property can be seized for tax purposes, settlement of lawsuits, and so forth.

For tax purposes, the sole proprietorship carries the greatest tax burden because it carries unlimited liability. The owner and business are one and the same for tax purposes, first to the business and second to the individual. Separate books must be maintained to separate the business income from your personal income.

The partnership form of business is perhaps better than the sole proprietorship. The partnership is a noncorporate form of ownership having two or more owners. It can be a general or a limited partnership. The basic difference between the two is that in the general partnership there is a general partner who has unlimited liability for debts and other obligations of the partners. In a limited partnership, a specialized group of partners invest their money and share in the profits of the business. Their liability, however, is limited to the amount of their investments. Taxes are paid by the individual partners on their share of the partnership taxable income.

The other major difference between the general and limited partnership is that a general partnership is established to conduct a business like making something and being able to decide what course of action to follow, which is often referred to as decision-making ability while a limited partnership is a means of investing money without decision-making authority, but your liability is limited to the amount of your investment.

The third basic form of conducting business is the corporation. Generally, there are two types of corporations: The C corporation and the S corporation. For tax purposes and nontax purposes, corporations are treated as separate entities. The basic difference between the C and S corporations is that the C corporation is the regular form of a corporation with taxes paid first by the corporation and second by the individual shareholders as dividends. This tax rule is often referred to as double taxation.

To get away from this double taxation, many small companies have set up corporations where incomes, deductions, losses, and credits appear to flow directly to individual shareholders. This eliminates the concept of double taxation because individual shareholders are responsible for their own tax liability based on what they earned or lost from the proceeds of the partnership. It is very similar to a modified partnership.

Corporations are generally the more acceptable forms of businesses due to limited liability, continuity of life, central management, and freedom to transfer ownership by buying or selling interest in the company. Stocks and bonds come into mind. You incur limited liability based on the amount of your investment in the business. You can lose all of your investments in the company if the company is doing badly and reap huge profits if it is doing well. The corporation has continuity of life in that one shareholder taking out all of their investments in the corporation cannot stop the corporation from existing because there are other shareholders to cover your withdrawals.

The centralized management is usually a board of directors with officers needed to render decisions and conduct business. Transfer of interest is done by the sale of stocks on the stock exchanges. This is where you can gain on your investment in the corporation or lose all of your investment in the corporation limited to the amount of your investment.

Generally, you establish a corporation to make money, but under some circumstances you establish a corporation not to make money but to provide some type of service like a church, club, civic organization, or some other group set up to perform some type of service. The monies that are received are used to run the organization and not to make a profit. Normally these organizations don't have to pay taxes.

To set up a corporation, an attorney is recommended, but it is not absolutely necessary. A good accountant is also recommended, but it is also not absolutely necessary. If you venture into this job on your own, you can obtain a C corporation kit at most stationery stores. With all of the legal forms you will need for filing, there are usually samples of completed forms with detailed instructions. If your business is serious enough for you to file as a corporation, you should get a lawyer and an accountant for professional help. You can do the paperwork, but it is much easier to get professional help to avoid some of the mistakes you can make by completing the filling yourself.

There are many things to consider when forming a corporation. The very first thing is to establish a name for the corporation. Generally a name is unique, identifies the purpose of the business, and does not conflict with another registered name listed with the Department of State in your state of incorporation.

One of the next things to consider is whether you will have a preincorporation and/or a subscription agreement. In the preincorporation agreement, things like the name, purpose, registered agent, place of business, duration of existence, board of directors, monies contributed, voting rights, and so forth are covered. You should get an attorney to help you with the documents. The subscription agreement involves how many stocks will be authorized, the price that subscribers will pay in addition to promissory agreements to purchase stocks, and the penalties to be imposed if agreements are not kept.

The articles of incorporation are then prepared for submission to the Secretary of State for approval or rejection. If it is accepted, corporate existence is effective with the date of delivery. Some states will issue a certificate of incorporation or send back a filing receipt indicating acceptance. New York, for example, sends back a filing receipt. Fees for filing may vary from state to state but is usually in the neighborhood of about $150.

Once the corporation is formed through the articles of incorporation, bylaws are prepared, a board of directors is elected, and meeting dates and places of meeting are established. The secretary of the board records minutes, maintains records, and keeps them filed in a permanent location for safekeeping. Meetings must be held at least once a year.

In essence, what I have given you is a brief synopsis of the business process. My intentions are not to replace the use of professional help in this process So by all means, get professional help if you desire. I know a little about this process because I set up a S corporation and a 501(c)(3) organization by myself.

Once you are up and running, you will need to obtain a tax ID number, prepare IRS and workmen's compensation forms, and establish a bank account. Generally, you will need to establish an account for the certificate of incorporation or filing receipt, proof of your tax ID number, a copy of the articles of incorporation, and your corporate seal, which can be obtained at a business stationery store for a modest fee.

How to Invest Your Money

W hat is worse than not having any money? To have money and then lose it because you did not know what to do with it. I am sure that you have heard of millionaires who lost everything because they did not have the right investment strategy. In this module, I will provide a safe and practical guide to investing, but as with everything else in life, investing is not an exact science, and you can lose everything and even go bankrupt.

But first, what is investing? Investing is acquiring assets or property rights to hold for a period of time to conserve capital or earn an income. When you put money in a bank, you are investing in that bank. You gain a deposit that you keep to conserve your money and to gain more money from interest received from the bank.

So the key to investing is the rate of return on your investment. How much interest will I gain for each dollar invested and for what period of time? For example, if you put $100 in the bank for a year at an interest rate of 5 percent, the following equation can show your return:

$$\text{Money earned} = \text{principal x rate x time}$$
$$M = 100 \text{ x } 5 \text{ percent x } 1 \text{ year}$$
$$M = 100 \text{ x } 0.05 \text{ x } 1$$
$$M = 5$$

In this example, you would have earned $5, which when added to your deposit would equal $105. If you received 8 percent on your investment, you would have received $8, and for 10 percent, you would have received $10. So you can see that I can start out with $100 and someone else can start out with $100 but end up with different amounts during the same period of time depending on the rate of return or the percentage. Therefore the key to investing is the rate of return on your investment. The higher the rate of return, the more your money grows and vice versa.

Banks and other financial institutions also use the system of compounding to determine how much and how quickly an investment grows. Compounding is difficult to explain, so I am not going to attempt to describe it at this time. In this module, the key thing to remember is that the greatest return results from the greatest percentage of interest on your investment.

The stock market has traditionally shown the greatest return while banks have shown the least. Therefore, putting your money in the bank does not always yield the greatest return, although it is the usually the safest, with little or no chance of losing your initial investment. In the stock market, you can lose all of your initial investment or part of it. This is the risk of trying to make more money than you can traditionally get from a savings account in a bank. Financial experts use a system of seventy-two to determine how money grows. They use seventy-two and divide it by the interest rate, and that number gives the number of years it takes for money to double.

For example, if the interest rate is 4 percent, divided into seventy-two yields eighteen years for your initial investment to double. If the interest rate is 12 percent, divided into seventy-two, the number of years would be six. If the rate is 10 percent, the number of years would be seventy-two. Therefore the key to investing is to get the largest return with the least chance of losing your investment.

To do this, we need to look at several means of investing, such as banks, real estate, stocks and bonds, mutual funds, and commodities. I will attempt to explain some of them and show you which offers the greatest return with the least chance of losing your money.

The first key to investing is to find out what investments yield the highest return with the least chance of loss. The second key is the use of compounding. After some research, I can explain compounding as it refers to interest rates as the amount of interest computed on an original interest, which is accrued and added to the previous amount over a period of time, such as daily, monthly, quarterly, or yearly.

Because of compounding, money grows in an inverse relationship to the period of time, therefore, the best method of compounding is daily followed by weekly, monthly, quarterly, and finally, yearly. Armed with this information, we can determine that the best method of investing is to gain the greatest rate of interest on your investment and combine that with the best method of compounding, which is daily, if possible. Since we now know that the best way to invest money is to attempt to gain the greatest interest rate compounded daily, if possible, let us turn our attention to some investment ideas.

Below are the different types of investments in banks with the number of years that it takes for initial investment to double:

1. Passbook savings—3 percent—24 years
2. Certificate savings—3 percent—24 years
3. Certificates of deposit (1 year)—5 percent—14.4 years
4. Money market accounts—5 percent—14.4 years
5. IRAs—6 percent—12 years
6. Mutual funds—9 percent—8 years
7. Checking accounts—1 percent—72 years

From this example, you can see that the greatest return on your money in a banking situation is mutual funds and the worst is a checking account.

Now let us examine the stock market. The best investment in the long run with the greatest rate of return is the stock market. It also offers the greatest risk. You can lose all or part of your money, so it is wise to know what you are doing. May God bless the fool! The stock market averages approximately 20 to 30 percent return on your investment, far outweighing anything in the bank. In the bank, however, your money is safe. The stock market is generally made up of common and preferred stocks.

Common stocks can be defined as residual ownership of a company. For example, when a company needs money to expand or buy assets, it sells a piece of the company for a specific price. In essence, they are borrowing money from you and depending on the success of the company. You can make money by the price of the stock increasing in value or from the company paying dividends. Some companies pay dividends; others do not. Dividends, when declared, are usually paid in cash or some other asset to the shareholders of the company.

Stocks are traded on the open market using discount brokers that are usually cheaper because they offer little or no advice. Full-service brokers are usually more expensive because they offer full advice and over-the-counter dealers who do not trade on a regular stock exchange such as the New York Stock Exchange. The three major exchanges are the NYSE, the Amex, and the NASDAQ.

Another investment tool is bonds, often referred to as securities issued by a company, obligating the company to pay the bondholder a specified amount of interest at specified intervals of time in addition to paying the bondholder the loan principal and its maturity value at the end of the agreed-upon time, which is referred to as the maturity date. In other words, you loan a company money for their use, and they agree to pay you interest at specified intervals. At maturity, you get back what you invested, including the maturity value. Bonds neither give you ownership nor voting rights, which are different from stocks on both accounts.

You get the right to invest, and your money is pretty much guaranteed to make a profit. Your return may not be as much as stocks when the market is going well, but they may be better in a real bear market. The advantage is that you have much less chance of losing your money than dealing with stocks, but the return is generally not as good. Bonds are usually classified as tax-exempt or non-tax-exempt. Non-tax-exempt generally pays the higher return because tax-exempt means you don't have to pay taxes, so your return is somewhat smaller. This is a good investment for someone who is looking for a tax shelter.

Since your initial investment is secure and you receive a profit on your investment that is pretty much guaranteed, bonds are an excellent investment because of this safety factor.

Mutual funds can be defined as several groups of stocks offered for sale with diversification built in. Some stocks in the fund may be high performing with high risk or low performing with less risk. In essence, you are dealing with a lot of companies instead of just one. The great returns can offset some of the lousy returns. Mutual funds are often classified as one of the very best investments and one of the safest. They average about a 10 to 15 percent return on your investment with little risk. For the beginner, they are perhaps the very best investment, especially if you select the right ones. For a few dollars, you can write or call me, and I will send you a list of the right ones.

Stock exchanges are used to provide a facility for the execution of customer orders. Stock brokers, brokerage houses, bond traders, and so forth are used as middlemen to bring buyers and sellers together in the execution of the orders. For performing this service, they are paid a commission. Stocks and bonds are the two best-known methods of investing in an organized exchange. Other methods of investing include trading precious metals such as gold, copper, and silver, which are referred to as futures, and trading agricultural products, such as wheat, corn, and soybeans, which are done on the commodity exchange. These methods of investing are highly lucrative but very highly risky. The ordinary investor should not consider them without professional advice.

In summary, there are many types of investments with the ultimate risk being the stock, futures, and commodities markets and the least being the banks.

The goal is to gain the greatest return with the least risk. For the beginner, the best investment strategy based on my research and my opinion would be investing in mutual funds followed by real estate, and when you become a little more advanced, tackle the stock market, starting with no-load mutual funds. As you progress, go full-fledged into the stock market with an emphasis on investing for the long term, because over the long haul, the stock market will outperform its competitors.

If you insist upon being adventurous in the beginning of your investment career and want to tackle the stock market, here is my formula for success:

1. Start with companies you know and deal with, in your everyday life, such as your supermarkets, drugstores, wholesale warehouse stores, telephone companies, clothing and appliance stores, computer stores, and places of employment using deferred compensation and 401(k) retirement plans.
2. Do research on these selections, concentrating on the cost of the stock in relationship to its earnings per share, sometimes referred to as its P/E ratio.
3. Stay abreast of what is happening in the news and business channels on these selections and update your selections as you progress.
4. Study the business pages of your local and national newspapers, such as the *New York Times* and the *Wall Street Journal*.
5. Buy the right company at the right price and try to avoid buying the right company at the wrong price, or the wrong company.
6. To ensure you buy the right company at the right price, pay attention to the fifty-two-week highs and lows listed in conjunction with the stock on the business pages of your newspaper. Always buy the best company when it is at or near its fifty-two-week low and sell when it is at its fifty-two-week high. Try not to buy the right company when it is at its fifty-two-week high, because it is usually ready to come back down. Nothing goes up forever.
7. Invest for the long haul. Don't pay too much attention to temporary bad news by stock analysts barely out of college who are suddenly experts. Study the company management concept and whether they are earning money and making a profit to determine how well it will grow before deciding to sell.
8. Buy good companies that are experiencing some bad news by the so-called experts known as stock analysts. Buy when the stock is going down and when it reaches a bottom. In other

words, buy when everybody is selling and sell when everybody else is buying. Demand, due to large volumes, often determines when to use this principle!

9. Stay away from the get-rich schemes. Anything that sounds too easy is usually very hard to accomplish unless you are extremely lucky. Be smart instead of lucky.

10. Paper trade for a few months using the above techniques until you gain a better understanding of how the system works.

11. Find yourself a good discount broker such as TD Ameritrade or Charles Schwab, and good luck. Unless you intend to use mutual funds or direct reinvestment plans as your investment tool, you will need about $5,000 to start you on your road to investing. Mutual funds can be started with as little as $1,000, and direct reinvestment plans can be started with as little as $100. You must be prepared to lose all or some of this money. It is okay to lose because it helps you to win by avoiding some of the mistakes that you make while losing.

12. Now that you have been armed with this information, research the names of companies to invest in, whether they are mutual funds, stocks, bonds, or direct reinvestment plans to begin your endeavor.

How to Learn to Read

R eading is fundamental. Either you know how to read, you can read in small portions, or you can't read. I am going to concentrate on those who don't know how to read or only read in portions. What I mean by reading in portions is people who are not illiterate but those who can read a little. A person who reads at a third-grade level can read a little, but perhaps not well enough to read the *New York Times* or the *Wall Street Journal* or complete an application for a job.

A person who cannot read at all is illiterate. They need assistance in dealing with problems involving reading but may be smart as a whip in everything else, so nobody knows they don't know how to read. There are millions of people who fall into this category. They are very proud people who don't want anyone to know they don't know how to read. I bet that if they were given a chance to learn without anyone knowing, they would jump at the opportunity.

The folks who fall into the category of knowing how to read a little would also jump at the opportunity to learn to read without anyone knowing. In this module, I will attempt to give you a chance to learn how to read in the privacy of your home without anyone knowing that you are. The method I will teach you is not very hard, but it takes diligence and effort, just like anything else in life that is worthwhile.

Learning to read involves a series of steps. In order to understand what I mean, you need to know what I mean by being able to read.

Reading, per my definition, is the ability to see a word and pronounce it, spell it, understand its meaning, and use that word in a sentence. For example, take the word *run*. If you saw this word written anywhere, you would know that it is spelled and pronounced r-u-n. It means to move at a pace much faster than walking. Here is an example of how it can be used in a sentence: "I am going to test you on how fast you can run around that track."

The opposite of run is *walk*. The same analogy can apply. Therefore, learning to read is the ability to see a word, spell it, pronounce it, know its meaning, and use it in a sentence. This definition is universal in any language you can think of. Learning to read is, therefore, the problem, and the solutions are based on the following steps.

The first step is to determine what phase of the equation you fall into. If you are illiterate, the methods I am teaching may be too difficult for you to use. Perhaps you need to throw away the shame and ridicule and get professional help by enrolling in some type of school. My method will work for you; however, it requires a great deal of time and persistence as well as a willingness to not give up, because if you don't give up, you cannot fail. A person only fails when they give up. This is true in all phases of life.

Once you establish what phase of the equation you are in, you are ready for the second step, which is to gather a lot of pencils, papers, and erasers. These items will become your tools of trade. A mechanic needs tools to repair a car; you need tools to learn to read. Pencils, papers, and a lot of erasers will forever be your tools of trade. A mechanic needs to know how to use tools to repair a car. You need to know how to use your tools to learn how to read.

The first thing you will be required to do is to make the following table. A table is nothing more than drawing some lines. Even if you are absolutely illiterate, you can still draw some lines. As you progress, your tables will become more expansive, but they will always remain in the same format centered around seeing a word, pronouncing it, spelling it, knowing its meaning, and using it in a sentence.

ALPHABET WORDS I USED PRONOUNCIATION SPELLING MEANING USED IN A SENTENCE

A
B
C
D
E
F
G
H
I
J
K
L
M
N
O
P
Q
R
S
T
U
V
W
X
Y
Z

Once you have drawn the above table, you are almost at the point of going to the third step in learning to read, beginning to use your tools. It is impossible to learn how to read without knowing the list of letters that every single word begins with, ends with, and uses in between. This list of letters is called the alphabet.

If you are building a house, you start with a foundation. Well, the alphabet is your foundation for learning to read. You cannot learn to read without knowing the alphabet. The letters of the alphabet have specific sounds that you will need to master before you learn to read. In the beginning, this is where you will spend the majority of your time, attempting to master the alphabet.

The first letter of the alphabet is *a*. The letter *a* is the beginning of your foundation. This is the first time that you will begin to use your tools. You will begin by practicing how to write the letter *a* using a pencil and a piece of paper. You will practice until you can make the letter *a* as perfect as washing your car or fixing your hair. You go on to *b* and *c* and so on until you can make every letter of the alphabet as perfectly as wearing your finest pair of shoes. This is all you do at the beginning. If someone told you to write the letter *z*, you would do so without even having to think. This simple step is the foundation for learning to read.

The alphabet is composed of capital letters and small letters. You have to practice each until it becomes as second nature as brushing your teeth or combing your hair. If you are illiterate, just this simple task might take you months or even years. I know how stupid this might sound, but if you remember you are beginning to read, you probably started out making the letters of the alphabet. It is an art that most people never mastered because they failed to take the time, effort, and energy necessary to master this art form, hence the very bad handwriting by many people in our society and the beautiful handwriting by others.

This simple procedure, however, is the basic foundation for learning to read and write. In the beginning, you should not move on to additional steps until you have mastered this one. Once you have mastered writing the alphabet, you are ready to begin learning how to pronounce each letter. This simple technique is the beginning of learning sound association, which becomes the basis for learning various forms of phonetics. There is nothing more important than memorizing the alphabet and the various sound of each letter of the alphabet. If you are able to master this phase of learning to read, then everything else will be easy.

To learn the alphabet and each letter's sound, you can use one of several methods. The best method is to see and hear someone pronounce the letters. The second method is to buy a tape of the letters and their sounds. Your children or grandchildren can help you learn how to pronounce and recognize the sounds of the alphabets. You could also get someone to make a tape for you with the letters and their pronunciations. You absolutely must memorize the letters of the alphabet and the sounds of each letter. Start with the letter *a* and don't move to another until you know how to write and pronounce the letter and you know the sound of the letter.

Once you know how to do this with each letter of the alphabet, you will find yourself almost at the point of being able to recognize and pronounce small words like *run, see, cat, dog, house, car, bus*, and so on. Before you know it, you will begin to recognize more and more words. Remember the table I had you to draw earlier? Well, you are now at the point of learning what to do with it.

You noticed the first column of the table dealt with the alphabet. Using this as the foundation for learning to read, you will now proceed to words you use in your daily living, like *cook, hair, eyes, teeth, clothing, shoes, stockings, paycheck, credit card, job, boss, cars, milk, money, sleep*, and tons and tons of other words. These are the words that will teach you how to learn to read, those you use in your everyday life. Learning how to recognize these words, pronounce and spell them correctly, know their meaning, and use them properly in sentences will teach you how to read. Many people use a word every day and would not recognize it if they saw it on a piece of paper and certainly would not be able to spell it. Oftentimes, they use it incorrectly in a sentence.

The words you use every day will become your foundation for learning how to read. The first thing you want to do is to make a list of every single word you use in your everyday life, like *house, car, loans, schools, park, shopping, work, sex, fight, church*, and so on. You can use the aforementioned table to sort these words in alphabetical order. You will need help in making this list.

A simple method to use is to associate a word with a product you use. Almost every product you use usually has its name on the label.

Start with this method. For example, *sugar*, *rice*, and *coffee* are spelled out on their bags. Use your children or grandchildren to help you with this list of words that will teach you to read. As you make this list, you will constantly add new words almost every day, terms you see on TV, hear on the radio, see on the back of the bus, and so on.

At this point, the difficulties start. You will be required to memorize, pronounce, spell, and recognize these words if you saw them somewhere. Other than if you saw them listed on the sugar bag, then you know it is sugar. If you saw the word *sugar* listed in a magazine, you would recognize the word. This tedious process requires a tremendous amount of diligence, but it will absolutely work to teach you how to learn to read. This method of learning to read and recognize words is based on the principle of sight and memorization. This method is slow and tedious, but it can be used in the privacy of your home and at your own pace.

You can take as long as you want, and nobody will ever know what you are doing. All you need to learn to read using this method are pencils, lots of paper and erasers, and an abundance of work, time, and patience. You will learn to see a word, pronounce it, spell it, write it, and learn its meaning and usages. This same technique can be used to learn any language. When you combine this method with phonetics, the study of sounds associated with words and parts of words such as prefixes and suffixes, and grammar, the study of the parts of speech and the various adaptations, you will become a real reader, someone who can read, understand, and comprehend.

If you review the aforementioned table, you will see that reading involves not only recognizing, pronouncing, and spelling words, it also involves learning the greatest gift of reading, which is learning the meaning of words and how to use them to communicate. Avid readers are usually excellent communicators, both orally and written. The basis for all learning is the ability to read, understand, and comprehend. If you are able to read very well, everything else will fall into place. This rudimentary module gives you a simple technique to teach yourself how to learn to read in the privacy of your home using your own abilities, but remember, the best way is to get professional help. Good luck.

How to Live in Peace

Will there be peace in our lifetime? Perhaps not because of the numerous differences among people. Although God created all of us as equal, we have yet to accept this fact. Instead of working on the commonality among people, we constantly search for the differences, the things that divide us. As Lincoln said, "A house divided cannot stand." Peace will come when we realize that we are one and the same, and until that happens, the world will never be at peace. We will continue to search for peace, which will never come. My goal in this module is to teach the world how to live in peace, starting with the greatest divider among humankind, religion.

Since the beginning of time, religion has been at the forefront of the problems among people. It continues even until today. If you look at the Middle East, the greatest differences among the people in this area center around religion. Although the ideology between Muslims and Jews may be slightly different, the major difference is in religion.

If you truly examine the two religions, you will see that they are very similar. In fact, all religions are very similar. In Northern Ireland, the many wars were fought over religion, although some folks would say that this was not true. If you examine these folks very closely, you will see that they are the same people. In fact, they fought all of these years over things that were so similar that if they had just stopped to review the similarities and work on them, perhaps there would have been no need for the many wars.

Look at what is happening in Serbia. The fight is over religion. These folks are the exact same people. In fact, family members may be of a different religion, and they are fighting among themselves. I would imagine if you examine every internal struggle within a country or tribe, you will see that the struggle is over religion. These folks are one and the same. Let us go all the way back to the Crusades. The fight was over religion, one nation trying to impose their religious beliefs on another nation of people when in actuality these folks were one and the same.

If people would stop and just examine the commonality between their adversaries and them, they will find that there are many more things that are exactly the same than things that are different. If they start with a base of commonality, place all the things that are common on one side of a piece of paper, and then place the things that are different on the other side, they will find that there will be very few things on the side of the paper listing the differences. In fact, if you try this simple procedure with all religions, you will find that this analogy is true.

If you examine every religion, there are three central themes. The first theme is that of a supreme being. That supreme being may be given different names in various religions, but it actually means the same. In Christianity, we call that supreme being "God." In Islam, that supreme being is called "Allah." In Buddhism, that supreme being is called "Buddha." In a tribal religion, that supreme being will have a name. If you are an Eskimo or Native American, you still believe in a supreme being. It might be called the god of the clouds.

The second central theme of every religion is that the supreme being is of the spirit. It is not human. You cannot see, hear, or touch this supreme being in a physical form, although you can feel its presence. If you travel all over the world, this analogy is evident within every single type of religion from the most primitive to the most sophisticated. This is also true from the beginning of time and continues even until today. It is believed that God, Allah, Buddha, or whatever name is used to describe this supreme being is of the spirit. Every religion also believes that to reach this supreme being, you must pray or talk to him in prayer or some type of communication, and you will receive an answer.

The third central theme of every religion is the belief in good and bad or good and evil. It may not be described in the terms of good and bad or good and evil in all religions, but it means the same thing. If you do right, you will be rewarded positively, and if you do bad, you will be punished. This belief even goes beyond our present existence and even into the hereafter.

Christians believe in heaven and hell. Native Americans believe in the big place in the sky or the clouds. If you examine every religion, they believe in some similar type of a value system. If you are good and love and treat your fellow human right, you will be rewarded, and if you commit evil or do something bad, you will be punished both in the present and hereafter. In all of the most advanced societies throughout history, they made elaborate preparations to prepare themselves for the journey into the hereafter. The Greeks, Egyptians, and Romans spent tons of money on elaborate preparations for their travel into the hereafter.

If you continue to list the similarities of each religion on one side of a piece of paper and the differences on the other side, the chances are very good that you will find that there are very few differences from a pure perspective. This leads me into the first criterion for being able to live in peace, to establish a universal religion or one religion for all of humankind. If this is done, there would be no need for fighting, persecution, or imposition of one nation's will on another. How can this be done?

Well, it is practically done already if nations come together and review the commonality of each religion and work toward achieving a commonality among the differences. This can be done by establishing a world council on religion where representatives from every nation, tribe, or village would be invited to work on the differences and reinforce the positives. The fact is that all religions are already built on a system that is good for humankind. The problem is that humankind does not practice what it preaches due to outside forces in our environment such as wealth, power, and influence.

Everybody wants to be rich; nobody wants to be poor, no matter what it takes. Peace can never be achieved; therefore because of the greed of one person over another and one nation over another, unless there is a total spiritual revolution, peace will never come. That spiritual revolution can only be achieved when humankind accepts the fact that we are all exactly the same. Skin color and all of that other nonsense that divides us must be eliminated. The ideal solution to this problem is the establishment of one true religion for all of humankind where wealth, power, and influence will not matter. It will only matter how closely you are affiliated with the supreme being of God Almighty.

True wealth should only belong to the people who have proven that they are worthy based on their affiliation with God Almighty. True believers in a true religion will know that poverty in the world should never be a consideration. There is no way that someone like Bill Gates, as an example, should be so rich that if he spent a million dollars a week, he would not be able to spend all of his money in a lifetime and have millions of children starving. Bill Gates, however, is doing an excellent job in helping to eliminate some of the problems in the world. I recently read that he is donating $750 million to various charities to fight the hunger problems in the world. He should be commended for this.

As I said, the first criterion for how to live in peace is through the establishment of one religion for all of humankind, and this leads me into the second criterion for how to live in peace, to free your mind.

Once you are able to free your mind, you will find that all people are exactly alike. Skin color and hair texture is so insignificant that it will have no real relevance. Let us proceed on how to live in peace using the technique of freeing your mind.

Freeing your mind is very difficult to do, but it is based on a simple principle called focusing. Have you ever seen 3-D drawings of different pictures? If you look at these pictures at a casual glance, you will not be able to see the picture that is illustrated. But if you look at these pictures long enough and focus very hard, your mind will lead you to the picture because it is painted or drawn in 3-D. When you free your mind through intense concentration, you will begin to see the picture. This is an example of what is meant by freeing your mind.

In order to free your mind to learn the first step in how to live in peace, you must focus all your energy on blanking out every possible stimulus in the world. This is almost impossible to do because every part of our lives is influenced by some outside force, whether it be religion, science, TV, radio, other people, sight, sound, and so on, continuing on into infinity. When your mind is free of all outside forces, you are then dealing with the heart.

When you free your mind of everything your heart can only reflect, good or bad, the thing that is unique about all people is that we are either good or bad. Once your mind is free, your heart will tell you whether you are good or bad. You will be able to judge people based on the content of their character instead of the color of their skin or the extent of their bank account. Hopefully, you will prove to be good because if you are bad, you will surely perish anyway. So I want to focus on those of us who are good in order for me to teach you how to live in peace. Remember, I said the first step is to free your mind. Now that leads us to the second step, to look from within at the outside world.

Now what the hell is Tom talking about, looking from within at the outside world? Well, this is what is meant. If you look from within at the outside world when your heart is good, you will see the outside world as good, and when your heart is bad, you will see the outside world as bad. Most people will see the outside world as bad because they are influenced by forces in nature such as power, money, success, fine cars, nice jewelry, big houses, swimming pools, and luxuries of all types and sizes. These people cannot be saved and will never be able to live in peace because of the fear of losing all of these luxuries.

In order to live in peace, you must be willing to give up everything or at least be willing to share everything with someone less fortunate. Rich people will never be able to see themselves without all of the trappings of wealth. They will always be miserable and unhappy because rich people are fearful of losing what they have. They practically hide from society out of fear that someone is attempting to get what they have instead on concentrating on giving it freely. When people are able to give up everything or at least share everything, then the world will be at peace. Every one of us wants to be rich; otherwise why would millions of people play lotteries and other games of chance?

When your heart is truly good and your mind is focused on the spirit, money and wealth have no real meaning other than "How much can I use my money to help someone other than my family?" Wealth should be used to help someone who is less fortunate. The real test for humanity is the willingness to give up or share everything because in actuality, everybody is your family. So, this leads me into the third step, to seek out your neighbor. Now what the hell does Tom mean by seeking out your neighbor?

To learn this, you need to know who your neighbor is. If you live in a house, your neighbor is the person next door or down the street. If you live in an apartment, your neighbor is also the person next door, down the hall, across the street, and so on. If you are homeless and sleeping in the park, there is another homeless person sleeping in the park. That person is your neighbor. In other words, everybody is your neighbor. You should be willing to do your best to help everybody, no matter whether they are family, friend, or foe.

So now that we know who our neighbors are, we can seek them out to offer help and assistance. You must talk to each other as well as visit, teach, and, above all, help one another. It does not matter whether they are black, green, purple, family, friend, or foe. Under all circumstances, you should be willing to help. If you believe in the Bible, you should love your neighbor as you love yourself.

Once we know our neighbors, this leads us into the fourth step for how to live in peace, to find out what is common between your neighbor and you. Every man, woman, or child in the entire universe has something that is common among them. That is, we all belong to the human race. We are all exactly alike. I don't care if you go to any part of the world, whether it is Africa, China, Russia, England, or anywhere else, you will find that every person is exactly alike.

Just think about it. Every person stands upright, walks on two feet, and has the same makeup. Every person has some type of skin color pigmentation, hair follicles, body parts, and so on. You have a penis. I have a penis. You have hair. I have hair. You have a nose. I have a nose. You have teeth, and I have teeth. I don't care if you are Jew or Gentile or rich or poor. You do the same things I do.

If you think even further, we do everything at about the same time. You may go for hours before you relieve yourself. I may go for hours before I relieve myself, but for sure at some point in time, you must relieve yourself. Think anywhere in the world. People are exactly the same. They do the exact same things in the exact same way. A man in Africa uses his penis to create life in a woman exactly the same as a man in Norway.

A woman in Turkey has a baby exactly the same way as a woman in South Carolina. So if you think totally rationally, everyone is exactly the same. People try to make us believe that skin color, hair texture, or intelligence make us different when in actuality, circumstances in our environment make us dissimilar. So Tom, why is the world so messed up if we are exactly the same?

The answer to that is very simple. Just think about it. If we all had nothing, then what would be different about us? The answer: nothing. People are different because the forces in the world cause us to be different. Some people have money and/or power. Others uses drugs. A few are religious fanatics. Some people are poor, homeless, motherless, fatherless, and/or childless. So the things that make us different are the qualities that some of us have that others don't.

Now what would make us the same? Remember, we are already exactly the same except for outside forces in the world. So in simple terms, the things that make all people different are the qualities that one person has that another person does not possess. This is common all over the world.

Since we established that all people are different because they are influenced by outside forces in the world such as war and poverty, money, and power, our goal is to make all people in the world exactly the same in spite of these outside forces. I believe that if everyone had the exact same things in life, such as life, liberty, and the pursuit of happiness, there would be no racism, wars, drugs, crime, hunger, education, money, government lobbying, religion, jobs, or medical problems.

If every person throughout the world had all the things that were needed instead of a few people owning everything and the majority of the persons owning nothing, there would be no need for stealing, lying, cheating, killing, and all other atrocities that are perpetuated in the world. Why is someone similar to Bill Gates having so much money that if he spent a million dollars a day it would take him more than a hundred years to spend all of his money? In fact, it has been calculated that it would take him something like two hundred years if he spent a million dollars a day. Why are little children starving all over the world when there are so many Bill Gates types of people?

Will there be peace in our lifetime? Perhaps not. If you are rich, you don't want to ever think about being poor, and if you are poor, you want to be rich but have long since accepted the fact that it is unlikely you will become rich. Peace will come when every human accepts another human as equal and when the rich make a concerted effort to rid the world of poverty and hunger through a serious sharing of their wealth. Unfortunately, God made all of us in His image, but humankind absolutely refuses to accept this divine principle of life. They are still trying to discover chromosomes that make us different instead of searching for the things in life that make us the same. When we accept the fact that all people are exactly the same in God's eyes, peace will come. That is perhaps never.

How to Lose Weight

In order to lose weight, you must set a goal. It is no different than anything else in life. Goals keep us on a level playing field and allow us to navigate that plain until we reach a desired result. When we set goals, we must think in terms of realistic goals. Losing weight is no different. The average person by the time they reach fifty years old has gained at least thirty pounds in extra weight.

When you consider that the average person starts to put on weight at around thirty-five, they gain about two pounds per year for fifteen years. Now think about this: If it takes you fifteen years to put on thirty pounds, what makes you think you can take off thirty pounds in two weeks and keep it off? The chances are good that if you use a crash diet to lose weight in a short time, you will put on the weight—and usually more—in an equally short time. Crash diets generally don't work for this and other reasons.

Weight must be taken off on a gradual basis over an extended period of time; therefore setting a realistic goal of maybe two pounds per month for twelve months is a more attainable goal. Further in order to set a goal, you need a reason to pursue it.

My goal when I first started to lose weight was to be able to look down and see my penis over a forty-six-inch waistline. Unless I had an unbelievably large penis, it was impossible to do. Your goal in losing weight might be related to some medical condition or desire to get into your wedding dress for your wedding anniversary. Whatever your goal might be, it is important to set one that is realistic and able to occur over an extended period of time. In this module, I will attempt to show you how to lose weight and keep it off. Unfortunately, it is effective, but it takes an extended period of time to complete. Don't get discouraged if it does not happen in two weeks.

The first step in losing weight is to establish an element of time. This is very difficult to do if you work and even more difficult to do if you commute a long distance to work. When you think in terms of the average person working eight to ten hours per day and commuting one to two hours per day to and from work, there is very little time left for trying to lose weight. Where do you find the time to lose weight when some form of exercise is necessary? If you leave home at 7:00 a.m. and return at 7:00 p.m., there is only twelve hours left in the day. If you sleep for eight hours, only four hours are left. If you cook, eat, help the kids with their homework, take a shower, prepare for bed, and set aside your clothes for work, there appears to be little time for exercising, especially when doing the laundry, washing the dishes, and making love to your spouse was not even considered. Reading and watching TV is nonexistent. The element of time is very important for losing weight, but where is the time? In actuality, there is none.

You must create the time. Losing weight involves diet and exercise. You can solve one element by not eating, skipping meals, or fasting, but where do you find the time for exercising when in fact you are so tired from going through a daily routine of work, kids, husband, wife, and homework? The last thing you want to do is to punish yourself with some dumb exercise. In fact, the element of time is the key reason why most people cannot lose weight. It is very difficult to find the time to throw in fifty push-ups and twenty-five sit-ups without cutting into your eight hours of sleep. If you want to jog or walk, it is even more difficult to get up at five in the morning to go jogging. It is too dark, cold, and scary. The same is true at night. You might go jogging and not come back based on some of the characters lurking around. So what is a person to do to find the necessary time for exercising?

Walking is perhaps one of the best and easiest exercises to do. It does not require any formal training, expertise, or special clothing except sneakers or comfortable shoes, and it can be done almost anywhere and at any time. Not only that, it is free for as much time as you need. Your lunch hour can be a perfect time for walking. It can easily be fit into any work schedule. You can organize a walking club at work or go at it alone. It is not even necessary to have a shower after walking unless you are doing an extremely brisk walk or jog.

When I first started to lose weight, this was my primary way of exercising. We had a walking club, and in one lunch hour, we could walk two to three miles with ease and return and change clothes and take a shower, if shower facilities were available. In fact, many companies have recognized the need for diet and exercise and installed cafeterias and exercise rooms in their facilities. Also there are many gyms and exercise salons all over the place with specialized rates for various personnel. Your lunch hour is an excellent time for establishing a daily exercise routine either by walking or jogging or using a regulated gym or exercise salon. Not only does it help you to keep the body fit, it helps you to keep the mind fit by eliminating stress and frustration.

Another lunchtime activity that can be used to offer some form of exercises are dance classes. Barn dancing, ballet, tap, and modem dance classes are offered at almost all hours of the day and sometimes can be fit into your lunch schedule or after-work schedule to get some much-needed exercise. In any event, you have to find creative ways to get exercise that doesn't adversely interfere with your everyday life and can be done on a regular basis.

Another simple technique for getting some type of exercise is to exercise while sitting at the table, moving your legs back and forth under the table. Also while taking a shower, you can do deep knee bends and push away from the shower walls. In fact, you can do some form of exercise while carrying out almost every form of your household duties from washing the dishes to doing the laundry. It is just a matter of thinking of a creative exercise to do and doing it. The bottom line, however, is that you absolutely must find the time for some type of exercise if you expect to lose weight and keep it off. Diet and exercise must become your way of life.

When I reviewed the various exercises that helped me to lose weight, I found that they were a "bitch" in the beginning, but your body appears to adjust to them, and before long, you start to feel bad if you don't do them. I have found that lifting weight is not necessarily a good way to lose weight because it tends to build muscle and muscles are heavier and appear to add weight to the body instead of reducing it.

Once you have lost some weight, however, it is a good thing to use weightlifting to firm up the flab that is left from the excess tissue. I am enclosing here my list of my favorite exercises. I have found them to be most beneficial early in the morning before you take your shower. Thirty to forty minutes per day is all you need to do at least four to five times per week to keep you fit and trim for life.

Exercising is just like drugs. Once you get hooked, you can't stop. Unlike drugs, however, it is okay if you don't stop. Before you start with any form of exercise, check with your doctor to see if there are any medical conditions that will prevent you from exercising. In the beginning, proceed in moderation and adjust as your body and mind become more comfortable as you go along.

Changing your eating habits is the other most effective and healthiest way to lose weight. Crash diets, diet pills, and over-the-counter "frails and shills" are not the way to go, however. I am not saying that they don't work because many do work very well, but over the long run, they are just like medication. Many do harm and good as well. Once you stop them, you tend to put back on more weight than you lose. In my opinion, they are an excellent means for a manufacturer to make money.

Changing your eating habits, from my definition, means to eat the exact same things you are currently eating but less of them. I am not asking you to do anything that you are not presently doing. If you like ice cream, then eat ice cream. If you like fried chicken, then eat fried chicken.

You see, the problem with diets is that they encourage people to eat a whole bunch of junk that they don't like, like rice cakes and wheat grass. At some point, you will stop eating that junk. Your body will adjust to two pork chops instead of four and three chicken wings instead of six because as you exercise and lose weight, your stomach will become smaller, and you can't eat as much anyway.

My other definition for changing your eating habits is to eliminate the foods that are not good for you. This definition is based on a biblical interpretation of what you should eat. It will go against many of the popular foods that all of us like, but I believe that if this definition were strictly adhered to from the beginning of time, all the weird diseases in the world would not exist. I know that humans will say that they are smart enough to process all foods to the degree that they will not be harmful. But I say that God is smarter than man, and if God says we should not eat these foods, then that is good enough for me.

This definition can be found in Deuteronomy (14:3–21 KJV). After reading these verses, I found that we should not eat the ox, sheep, goat, heart, roebuck, fallow deer, wild goat, pager, wild ox, chamois, and every beast that parted the hoof, cleaved the cleft into two claws, and chewed the cud.

> Nevertheless, these you should not eat of them that chew the cud, or of them that divide the cloven hoof; as the camel, and the hare, and the donkey; for they chew the cud but divide not the hoof; therefore they are unclean to you. And the swine because it divide the hoof but it does not chew the cud. It is unclean unto you. You should not eat of their flesh nor touch their dead carcass. Further these you shall eat of all that are in the waters: all that have fins and scales shall you eat. Whatsoever that don't have fins and scales you should not eat because they are unclean to you. Of all the clean birds you shall eat. You should not eat the eagle, the ossifrage and the osprae, the glede and the kite and the vulture, raven, owl, night hawk, the cuchow and hawk, little owl and great owl and the swan and the pelican, great eagle and the cormorant, stork, heron, lapwing and bat. And every creeping thing that fly is unclean to you. You should not eat anything that dies of itself and

you should not seethe a kid in his mother's milk. Based on the passages from the bible the things that jump out at you that we should not eat are pigs, shrimps, scallops, crabs, clams, oysters, catfish, eel and other fish that don't have fins and scales because they are unclean.

The pig is unclean because its hoof is split, but it does not chew the cud. Forget about spareribs, pork chops, and bacon. Forget about shrimps, lobsters, oysters, crabs, and all other fish that don't have fins and scales. Imagine if we had abided by these teachings. Perhaps there would be a lot fewer incurable diseases in the world, things like cancer, heart disease, and strokes.

If you really want to change your eating habits and improve your health, eat as God commanded His children in their exodus from Egypt. Stay away from pork, shrimp, lobster, crab, and any other fish that doesn't have scales and fins. In addition, eat lots of fresh fruits, vegetables, nuts, and whole-grain cereals. Stay away from processed foods using heavy saturated fats and salt.

If you continue to eat the right blends of fresh foods and avoid pork and fish that don't have scales and fins, not only will you be much healthier, your weight will always be in alignment with your mind and body.

The final criterion for losing weight is a change of your mind-set. Losing weight is like anything else. In order to do it, you must believe that it can be done and must be willing to take the steps to do it. Unfortunately, this is very difficult because eating works on the pleasure principle. It is enjoyable. The first date you go on is to a movie and then dinner. What is nicer than going out to dinner and having someone serve and pamper you?

The hardest part to losing weight is to change your mind-set. Unless you can separate food from pleasure, it is difficult to lose weight. Every time you think about food, you need to do a refocusing of your thought process and say, "I don't want that pork chop sandwich."

There are perhaps more commercials on TV focusing on food than anything else. Their goal is to get you not to change your mind-set.

Kraft foods would go out of business if everyone wanted to be skinny and were able to control their appetite. Unfortunately the opposite is true because there are a lot more overweight people than skinny ones. Changing your mind-set takes tremendous control. Not only must you be able to change your mind-set concerning food, you must also change your mind-set concerning exercising.

Every day that you don't want to get out of the bed to exercise, you must convince yourself to do it. Changing your mind-set takes a tremendous amount of energy to ward off the desires for food and the dislike of punishing your body for exercising. Until you can do this, you will continue to be like I am, a short, fat man searching for a dream. Keep the faith, baby. Diet, exercise, and a change of mind-set will do the trick. After about two years of hard work and dedication, you will see some results.

How to Make a Cheesecake

Eating disorders—including obesity and anorexia—are very common in our society. News stories flash every day showing famous movie stars involved in serious weight loss episodes attempting to lose weight because of some particular movie role and models so undernourished that they look like they went through a famine. It is no wonder that tons of cookbooks and diet secrets are leading opportunities to make money. People like Oprah Winfrey and many others have been in the news about losing weight and regarding weight gain and weight loss problems.

Why is the world so fascinated with the question of weight? Nobody wants to be fat. Is it because you look awful or it affects your health? Does being too skinny also affect your health? Probably so! Since nobody nowadays wants to be fat, I have decided to do a module on how to make a cheesecake for those fat enthusiasts who don't care if all the models are as skinny as a rail. I don't have a problem with being fat, especially if your health is not affected. Sit back and relax, and follow my guide on how to prepare a cheesecake.

The first thing you need to know is the definition of a cheesecake. The noted authority, Mr. Webster, states a cheesecake is a dessert cake made from cream cheese, cottage cheese, eggs, and sugar, which may be topped with a variety of fruits. Based on this definition, it appears that if you throw all of this stuff together, mix it, and toss it in the oven, then you have a cheesecake.

Well, it is not quite that simple. It would probably work, but unless you know what you are doing, it is like driving a Chevy compared to a Mercedes. The key thing here is to know what you are doing, like how many eggs, how much sugar, and so on. You get the picture. Now let us proceed.

There are generally four steps in preparing any cheesecake. The first step is to get the correct equipment. Just like a mechanic needs the right tools to repair a car, you need the correct tools to make a cheesecake. The first thing you need is a springform pan. It is used for baking your cheesecake. The springform pan is easier to get the cake out of the pan once it is baked. Any pan can be used, but the springform pan just makes it a little easier to remove the cheesecake. The second thing you will need is a set of mixing bowls, at least one small one for the crust and a large one for mixing the fillings. In addition, you need an inexpensive mixer generally with a low and high speed. Once you obtain these tools, you are ready to prepare any type of cheesecake.

The second step is to prepare the crust for aligning the bottom of your springform pan to form the base for the cheesecake. The key ingredients for the crust are sugar, margarine, and the mix itself. Some folks like to use graham cracker mix, the simplest of all mixes. I like to use a combination of graham cracker mix combined with vanilla wafers and ginger snaps. These three mixes together give the crust an excellent base and quite an exquisite taste as well.

To prepare the crust, you will need approximately one cup of graham cracker mix, a half cup of vanilla wafer mix, and a half cup of ginger snap mix, along with one-fourth cup of sugar (regular or brown sugar if you prefer), one-fourth cup of soft margarine, and one tablespoon of evaporated milk. Using a small or medium bowl, mix these ingredients together for a few minutes and then spread the base at the bottom of the springform pan. Once you have done this, you are ready to proceed with the third step, to prepare the filling.

When preparing the filling, once you get beyond the basic ingredients of cream cheese, cottage cheese, and/or sour cream, sugar, and eggs, you can become quite creative with other ingredients. In fact you can throw in almost anything you want, from cookies and cream to fruits and nuts.

Personally, I like to stick with the basics along with sautéed bananas. To complete the filling, I recommend using at least two or three eight-ounce packages of soft cream cheese, one cup of cottage cheese, one cup of sour cream, one and one half cups of sugar, three eggs, two teaspoons of vanilla extract, one teaspoon of cinnamon, one quarter teaspoon of nutmeg, and the juice from two sautéed bananas. (This cream cheese is my own special mix and is called a banana sunrise.)

Using a large mixing bowl and an electric mixer, mix these ingredients for approximately two to three minutes until they become a smooth, creamy solution. Once this is done, empty the contents evenly into the springform pan and place it in an oven preheated to 325 degrees or slightly lower if you are not quite sure about the oven temperature, but never more than 325 degrees. Don't open the oven until approximately fifty-five minutes, at which time you slightly touch the middle of the cake to see if it springs back upon touch. If it does, the cheesecake is done. Remove it and let stand at room temperature for one hour.

If it does not spring back upon touch, reduce the oven temperature to 300 degrees and cook it for another ten minutes. Remove it at this time and let it stand at room temperature for one hour. Once the cake has cooled, it should be covered and placed in the refrigerator for chilling. Generally, cheesecakes are prepared for use as desserts for the following day because they need to be chilled overnight.

Oftentimes during cooking, your cheesecake will crack. This is normal. Sometimes it can be avoided by a slight reduction in the cooking temperature. In any event, your creative topping will cover up the cracks.

While your cheesecake is cooking or after it is completed, you can work on the last step in the preparation of a cheesecake, to prepare the topping. Toppings can come in a variety of forms. Generally they can be of the baked variety or a pour-over variety. If you are going to use a baked variety, remove the cake just before it is done and pour the topping over the cheesecake and return it to the oven for another three to five minutes for it to settle in. Just like the filling, you can use your imagination for the topping. Almost any conceivable varieties of whipped cream, sour cream, or fancy fruit toppings can be mixed and poured over your cheesecake.

In my special banana sunrise cheesecake, once the cheesecake has been chilled overnight, I blend the following as my special topping: the whites of three eggs, one teaspoon of sugar, a touch of cinnamon, one-quarter pound of red seedless grapes, and two bananas blended until creamy smooth. And then I pour it over the chilled cheesecake and bathe it with whipped cream. Once this is done, I return it for chilling for another ten minutes before serving.

Cheesecakes can be an assortment of elaborate desserts designed for a person with a sweet tooth. They are not very difficult to prepare, and there are numerous recipes for its preparation. The foregoing module describes a simple technique that anyone can follow to prepare the basic components of a cheesecake, that is, the crust, the filling, and the topping. Slight variations can be used to fit your individual and specialized taste.

How to Negotiate Successfully

T he art of negotiation is a skill that all of us need in our everyday lives. What happens when you go into a car dealership and try to purchase a vehicle for less than the sticker price? You are negotiating. How successful you will be depends on your skills at negotiating. The dealer wants you to pay the full price, but he knows there is a lesser price that he will accept. Your goal is to get him to settle at the rock-bottom price. How you do this is what this module is about.

There are some interesting techniques to follow to find out the rock-bottom price. Not only is this true when it comes to purchasing a car, it is true with everything else in life. When you go on a job interview, you are negotiating for a position with the company at a particular salary. The salary being offered may not be the highest salary that you can receive for your services. How successful you are at negotiating and selling your ability to help the company may indeed garner you a few extra thousands in salary. Our goal, therefore, is to learn the secrets of a successful negotiator. Hopefully, this module will help you in this endeavor.

Negotiation is the exchange or communication of information between two or more persons attempting to reach some type of agreement. Usually this process involves two people with different positions in the process and must achieve a meeting of the minds to reach an agreement. Jesse Jackson has made a reputation of being an effective negotiator by securing the release of American hostages on several occasions. He was able to reach an agreement, even under hostile environments, which is often very difficult to achieve. It is difficult to effectuate an agreement in a hostile environment, so it is important to establish an environment of mutual respect. This is true in almost any type of negotiating process from making an offer on a house to negotiating a job offer or a salary increase.

From this perspective, the first thing you want to do as the client is to establish a good rapport between the interviewer and you. You can establish the rapport by commenting on something that the interviewer might be wearing, like a nice tie or a beautiful suit. Also commenting on things like pictures on the desk or paintings on the walls are a good method to use as well. A tasteful joke might also do the trick if the person appears to have a sense of humor. Once you hae established the rapport, you are ready to begin the process of how to negotiate successfully.

The very first thing you want to do in the negotiating process is to establish what you want to achieve. Without some semblance of what you want, it is almost impossible to reach a decision. You must establish your personality trait to determine if you can reach an agreement in the negotiating process. For example, some people are skeptical of everything and afraid to make a decision. If you gave them the world, they would still not believe it and would want to give it back, and others are so gullible that you can sell them anything. Someone like an accountant might be so methodical and precise that you cannot give them enough information without them wanting more and more information before they are able to reach an agreement.

Knowing your personality trait is therefore very important in becoming a successful negotiator. Once you have established your personality trait, you are ready to proceed with the actual process of you as the client and the other person as the interviewer. During the entire time of the negotiation process, you must always be willing to listen attentively to what is being said instead of just hearing what is being said. Listening is the key.

Oftentimes the interviewer will use the technique of intimidation to impose their will on you. It is difficult to negotiate out of fear and emotions because these will cloud your thinking. You will cave in much quicker if you are fearful and lose control. The key thing is to maintain eye contact and a self-assured body language. Sit or stand erect, and don't slump down in the chair when someone is using intimidation. Speak forcibly without shouting, and the interviewer will immediately know that you are not fearful to negotiate and cannot be intimidated. If you are prepared and confident in your abilities, it is difficult to be intimidated, which leads me to the first criterion for being successful as a negotiator, to be prepared. You must do your homework. Know the facts, and half the battle is won.

For example, if you went to purchase a car and the sticker invoice shows a specific price, you know already that there is a dealer's invoice for that car with a substantially lower price. Ask to see the dealer's invoice and negotiate from that price. Another example is if you found a house that you are prepared to buy and you want to make an offer. You know already the listed price is rarely the selling price on a resale house. Houses generally sell within 5 to 10 percent of its market value.

Ask the realtor to prepare a comparative market analysis of recent home sales in that area for you to assess before making an offer. In addition, you know already that closing costs, although mainly paid by the buyer, can be negotiated between the buyer and seller. Often the seller is willing to help you with the closing costs or may be willing to enter into a seller's concession or contribution if this is the only way to allow you to buy the house, especially if you are qualified and meet all other conditions.

In other words, to be an effective negotiator, you must be prepared by knowing the facts and the various parameters to help you reach an agreement with the interviewer. Being prepared means doing the necessary research because the more knowledge you have about a particular subject matter, the less chance you have of receiving the short end of the negotiating process.

This leads me into the second step in becoming a successful negotiator, to ask good questions. Good questions come in two forms. The first is based on your competence in the subject matter, which comes from being prepared. The second is based on closing or open-ended questions. Closing or open-ended questions paint a picture that requires a response. A simple example would be you are a prospective buyer of a house and ask the seller, "If I am prepared to close the deal immediately, will you accept my offered price?" In this example, the seller is forced to make a decision.

Another example might be to a prospective car dealer, "I am willing to make the purchase if you are willing to give me a three-year warranty on parts and service instead of two years." If the dealer can deliver the extra year, you are ready to make the deal.

The third step in how to become a successful negotiator is to negotiate for benefits as well as price. This is especially true when it comes to employment. An excellent benefit package is often worth a lot more than a few thousands in additional salary. Things like full health and dental coverage for all family members, stock options, annual performance bonuses, matching 401(k) contributions, or guaranteed cost of living adjustments are much more important than an extra $5,000 in salary. In fact, it has been shown that an excellent benefits package can be worth as much as $40,000 to $50,000 in additional salary, especially when one serious illness can wipe out your entire fortune.

The fourth step in how to become a successful negotiator is to understand the price allocation system. In the business world, there are two prices that a businessman is faced with: the costs of goods and services and the selling price of goods and services to determine if a profit can be made in addition to the expenses for making the goods and services. In order to ensure a profit, you must be able to sell your goods for more than it costs to make the goods, including materials, labor, and expenses of advertising. Oftentimes goods are marked up as much as 1000 percent to ensure that a profit is made. So when a sale is used to sell the product, chances are still excellent that a substantial markup is still evidenced beyond the actual cost of the product.

Don't feel bad for the clothing store when you buy a pair of shoes for $40 when the original price was $70. A good negotiator never pays the original cost for clothing, shoes, appliances, and so on. Even the sale price is higher than what you should pay. A person in business is willing to accept less than the asking price if they want to remain in business. Always attempt to purchase anything that you buy at a price less than the asking price.

A good rule of thumb with big-ticket items like houses, cars, appliances, and other big-ticket items is to offer 20 to 30 percent less than the asking price and hold firm in your offer. Don't be a fool, however, because you must be realistic when the item is priced within 5 percent of its market value. Make every effort to find out the market value before reaching a final decision.

This leads me into the final step in how to negotiate successfully, to be willing to compromise and make a decision. If you are a skeptic or a person who is so precise in your convictions, it is difficult to compromise and make a decision because of your insecurity. At some point in the negotiating process, you will reach either an agreement or a stalemate. An agreement is what you want to achieve if both parties are serious in the process. An ideal meeting of the minds is when the client feels that they got less than they should have gotten and the interviewer feels they gave up more than they should have given up.

This is especially true in the real estate business when it comes to the buyer and seller. The seller thinks he sold for too little, and the buyer thinks he bought for too much. This is perhaps the ideal selling price. The realtor who can bring about this scenario has done an excellent job. In order to compromise and make a decision, you need to re-evaluate your objectives to determine what you want. Do you want the house or not? You must be willing to look at the big picture. If you cannot, you will always be saying "I would" or "I could, but I didn't." A good negotiator knows when it is the right time to circle the wagons and be willing to compromise and make a decision to bring about closure, which is the final step in the process.

In summary, to become successful as a negotiator, you must know how to establish an objective based on your personality trait and listen instead of hearing to what is being said. In addition, you must be as prepared as possible, ask questions about everything you don't understand, and be rational enough in your thought process to compromise and make a decision to bring closure to the negotiation process.

How to Repair Bad Credit

Credit is the key to getting what you want in life. The lack of credit works just the opposite. Although it is still possible to get the things you want without credit, it is much more difficult. There is just no way that you can buy big-ticket items like houses, cars, and boats without credit unless you are rich and can afford to pay for everything in cash. This appears unlikely since 90 percent of the wealth in this country and perhaps the world is owned by 10 percent of the population. Unless you fall in that 10 percent, the chances are extremely good that you will need credit to buy the things that you want in life. You can't wait until you save all the money that you need to purchase a house with cash. It is almost a certainty that you will need to obtain a mortgage to purchase a house, and this can only be done if you have good credit.

Therefore, it is really a shame for someone to ruin their credit and be classified as a poor credit risk. Unfortunately college students often fall into this category by refusing to pay student loans and credit cards. They finish college with a degree and obtain a good job but are unable to purchase a simple thing like a car without their parents' help or by using a cosigner. Studies have shown that more than 60 percent of college students have poor credit by abusing credit cards, cellular phones, pagers, student loans, and so on. These folks are behind the eight ball even before their lives have begun. This is truly a shame.

In this module, I will show you various methods of repairing your credit after it has been ruined. I am sure there are many other methods that can be used in conjunction with the methods I will teach, but key to the whole thing is to do something to repair your credit after it has been ruined. You will know that your credit is ruined when you attempt to purchase something on credit and get turned down even though you have a good job. It is rather embarrassing when you attempt to purchase that dream car and are told, "Sorry, based on the information obtained from a credit agency, we cannot give you this car." You are forced to lie by saying to your friends, "I decided to wait because I did not want to deal with those high monthly payments." How to solve this problem is what this module will attempt to do.

The very first thing you need to do is find out what is on your credit report. You can get a free credit report from TRW by calling them and enrolling in their services, or you can obtain a credit report from a local real estate office, bank, mobile home sales office, or some other financial institution. The cost may vary from nothing to as much as $25.

There are various levels of bad credit. The very worst are collection accounts, charge-offs, judgments, foreclosures, and bankruptcies. The least are thirty, sixty, and ninety days late. The worst are very difficult to repair and offer the greatest chance of a person not being able to obtain additional credit. The only possible way to obtain additional credit with judgments and charge-offs is to contact the companies and/or the legal entities and make arrangements to pay off the outstanding debt. Oftentimes there are legal fees and other fees associated with judgments and charge-offs. These fees must be paid as well.

Once a company is contacted, that company may be willing to negotiate a settlement that may be less than the outstanding amount owed. You can only determine this by taking the initiative to contact the company. Once you pay off the agreed balance, you must obtain a release from the judgment for filing in the county clerk office where you live. This procedure is required to remove the judgment from your record. Charge-offs are very similar to a judgment. Usually a company, after making every effort to collect a debt, writes it off as a bad debt expense and considers the person a deadbeat. Charge-offs can be removed by contacting the company, arranging to pay off the outstanding balance and obtaining a letter of satisfaction indicating the debt was paid. Collection accounts are usually the first step a company uses to collect a debt that a person refuses to pay.

Collection companies are set up to follow up on bad debts with the goal of collecting the debt, and for their services, they obtain a percentage of the monies owed. Once an account has been referred to a collection company, you have to contact that company to make arrangements to pay off the debt, along with certain legal fees. Oftentimes these companies are willing to negotiate a lesser amount if you agree to pay off the debt immediately or in a reasonable time.

In every instance, you should get a letter from the company attesting that the debt was paid off. Once a company referred your debt to an outside agency like collection companies, attorneys, and so on, you usually have to contact the referral agency to make restitutions. These agencies usually get paid based on a percentage of the monies collected. The key thing in this entire process is to make contact and make arrangements to pay off the debt and obtain a letter attesting that the debt was paid.

After you have paid off an outstanding balance, the next course of action to follow is to follow up with the credit reporting agencies to remove the adverse report on your credit profile. There are three major credit reporting agencies: TRW, TransUnion, and Equifax. Each of these agencies must be contacted to do this. I would strongly suggest that you send them a certified letter returned receipt requested along with a letter asking them to remove the adverse report on your credit profile. You must include the release from judgment or the satisfaction letter to prove that the debt has been settled.

The biggest reason why people have poor credit is that they fail to use early intervention. You can avoid credit problems by using the technique of early intervention. What this means is that you must contact a company in the earliest stage of the problem.

Immediately when you know that you will not be able to make a payment at the time it is due, you should contact the company to let them know your intentions. This shows a company that you are concerned, and they are usually very understanding and willing to cooperate. The other technique to eradicate credit problems is to contact the company to arrange reduced payments or change the payment due date. Companies are always willing to help you keep your credit profile in order because it saves them the hassle of having to pursue collection remedies.

Using these techniques of early intervention will allow you an opportunity to leave your credit profile in good order and avoid the scenario to the thirty-, sixty-, and ninety-day late payments. A few thirty days late and even sometimes one or two sixty days late will still get you additional credit but very often at a higher interest rate, which is better than not being able to obtain credit at all.

Foreclosures and bankruptcies are an entirely different ballgame. Once you get to this point, you are like a fish out of water. Eventually you will die. Your goal is to always avoid this problem using early intervention either by your own means or through the means of the many credit repair companies that are cropping up all over the place, even on the internet. Even if you got to the level of a foreclosure, which is the loss of property due to a forced sale resulting from a court action for failure to make mortgage payments, your life is not entirely over.

A bankruptcy is a legal remedy whereby your property is divided among your creditors through a court order filed in a bankruptcy court, and from this process, you obtain a relief from your creditors either through arrangements to pay them off or full relief if you cannot pay them off. This process, in effect, gives you a fresh start but at a seriously high price. Foreclosures and bankruptcies are the ultimate price to pay in the ruination of your credit. They can practically follow you around for life. Neither one, however, is the end of the world. You can still obtain credit perhaps by the use of a security arrangement or a collateral arrangement.

For example, many companies will allow you to reestablish credit by issuing you a secured credit card. What it means is that you deposit a certain amount of money in their financial institution, and the company will issue you a credit card usually at least in the amount of your deposit and oftentimes one and a half times or two times the amount of your deposit. If you maintain an excellent credit profile from this point for at least two to three years, you can again be a model citizen.

As you can see, there is nothing more important than maintaining good credit. Once your credit is ruined, the difficulties in transacting financial business is immense. That is, you can usually avoid many problems by using the technique of early intervention, early contact with your creditors to arrange reduced payments, changes in payment dates, or some other remedy. Oftentimes maintaining good credit can be done at a personal level by an individual using the techniques mentioned in this module, but it is not intended to avoid using professional help of attorneys and credit-servicing agencies. If you think you need credit counseling, by all means get the help that you need. It can only save you some embarrassment in the future.

How to Set Up a Budget

Every organization needs financial stability to exist. Budgets play an important role in this endeavor because there would be total chaos without some type of financial order. Bills would not be paid, checks would bounce, and governments would collapse because you would never know what expenses are outstanding and what income is left to handle the expenses. Budgets are used as a guide to maintain order because income should be greater than expenses for an organization to remain solvent and not have to borrow from some source to remain solvent.

For example, you make $400 per week. Your expenses should not be more than $400 per week. If your expenses are more than $400, then you have a deficit, and if it is less than $400, you have a surplus. In other words, income equals expenses. People start to run into problems when their income is less than their expenses. Hello, credit card. They must revert to borrowing to make up the difference.

Everybody talks about a balanced budget, and in simple terms, all it actually means is that income equals expenses. The federal government derives their income from taxes, and you derive your income from working or some other source that is hopefully legal. The federal government has expenses, and hopefully their income will equal their expenses, but it never does. Therefore the budget is never balanced, and they are running a deficit of millions of dollars.

The same simple principle applies to an individual. You work and receive an income. You pay your rent, buy food, pay your bills, and save a few dollars, and hopefully these expenses don't exceed your income because if it does, you also have a deficit and must revert to borrowing to remain solvent.

As you can see, a budget is crucial in maintaining a sense of order and stability, for without one, keeping your finances in order would be challenging indeed. To highlight the seriousness of an inadequate budget or to not have one in place, the following excerpts appeared in the *Washington Post* on or about November 12, 1995.

> President Clinton and Republican leaders failed to arrange a meeting yesterday aimed at averting a shutdown of the federal government. At issue is a short-term spending measure that would keep the government operating after midnight tomorrow when current funding runs out.

You know that if a budget is important enough to the federal government to consider shutting down the government, it is certainly important enough to an individual to have one in place and stick to it. If an individual does not have a good budget in place and sticks to it, that person will end up with a very poor credit history or even bankruptcy because borrowing to stay afloat can only go so far before the bubble bursts and you are unable to pay your bills because your bills are greater than your income and all of your available credit has been used up.

In this module, I will show you how to set up a budget and give you some tips on how to keep your income equal to or greater than your expenses so that borrowing will not be necessary. The very first thing you need to do is to make a list of every single thing you spend money on and put it down on paper or in your computer. Your list might look like this.

EXPENSES	NECESSARY	BUDGETED	SPENT
1. MORTGAGE/RENT	YES	$900	$900
2. UTILITIES	YES	$150	$140
3. PHONE	YES	$125	$140

EXPENSES	NECESSARY	BUDGETED	SPENT
4. CREDIT CARDS	NO	$300	$500
5. CABLE	NO	$65	$70
6. CAR PAYMENT	YES	$500	$500
7. CAR INSURANCE	YES	$280	$280
8. CAR EXPENSES	YES	$175	$65
9. GROCERIES	YES	$500	$600
10. CLOTHING/CLEANING	MAYBE	$200	$180
11. LIFE INSURANCE	YES	$230	$230
12. ENTERTAINMENT	NO	$200	$225
13. CHARITY	NO	$100	$100
14. GYM/CLUB	NO	$0	$0
15. MEALS OUT	NO	$150	$210
16. SAVINGS	YES	$200	$100
17. COLLEGE	YES	$560	$560
18. CHILD CARE	MAYBE	$0	$0
19. RETIREMENT	MAYBE	$125	$0
20. SCHOOL LOANS	YES	$250	$250
21. ALIMONY	MAYBE	$0	$0
22. CHILD SUPPORT	MAYBE	$0	$0
23. PARENTAL SUPPORT	MAYBE	$0	$0
24. COMPUTER SUPPLIES	NO	$0	$25
25. EXTRAORDINARY MEDICAL	MAYBE	$200	$250
26. INVESTMENTS	NO	$100	$40
27. ADULT EDUCATION	NO	$0	$0
28. SUMMER CAMP	NO	$0	$0
29. VACATION FUND	NO	$50	$60
30. MISCELLANEOUS	MAYBE	$0	$140
TOTALS		$5,360 x 12 = $64,320	$5,565 x 12 = $6,6780

In this example, you can see that our budget is not in balance. In fact, we have a budget deficit of $205 per month, which translates to

$2,460 per year. Now let us examine some of the items listed in the budget to see if they can be reduced or eliminated.

This budget makes the assumption that your monthly income is reflective of what you used to establish the budgeted amount. The first thing listed in this budget that you might not need or you can reduce are credit cards. Many credit cards have an annual percentage rate of 18 to 25 percent. There are also many with a rate of 12 to 15 percent or even less. If you shop around, you can usually find a card with a lower rate than the ones you are using. You can transfer balances from the high-rate credit cards to the lower ones. This could save you hundreds of dollars per month.

The very best plan, however, is not to use credit cards at all. You can use layaway plans to make the purchases that you don't need immediately or wait until you have sufficient money to make the purchase. It is rare that the thing that we bought using a credit card was an absolute necessity. The chances are good that it was a hasty decision that probably did not make very much sense. The other thing is if you must use a credit card, pay off the entire balance each month to avoid paying finance charges. If you are unable to do this, then you should always pay more than the minimum payment to help reduce finance charges.

Another item in your budget that can usually be reduced but certainly not eliminated is the amount of money spent on food. You can save a lot of money using discount coupons and buying store brands. In addition, you can take advantage of the two-for-one sales and buying the larger-size items, which is usually cheaper per pound or ounce. Also different cuts of meats can vary considerably in price. For your fresh fruits and vegetables, you can buy them at wholesale prices at your local farmers' market in addition to growing them in your gardens. Not only is this rewarding, it is very healthy. I am sure that you can think of many other means of reducing your grocery bill that, when taken collectively, can save you hundreds per month.

Nowadays almost all clothing can be machine-washed and are made of some fabric that does not require dry cleaning. If you follow the instructions for care of the garments on the labels, you will probably reduce your dry cleaning bills in half. As far as the purchase of new clothing, you can save tons of money by buying clothing at the end of the season when they have been marked down to get rid of them to make room for the new merchandise. You can save as much as 25 to 75 percent using this method.

The cost of dining out and other forms of entertainment can put a heavy dent in your budget. It is almost impossible to go to a nice play and have dinner in the same evening. Just the cost of a movie for you and your guest can be expensive. A sporting event is unbelievable. To keep your budget at a reasonable level, you must go to the theater using discount tickets and at times that are atypical for the industry. For dining out, more and more people are using places that offer buffet style, all-you-can-eat menus. They are usually a little less and offer some variety for a reasonable price. For the moviegoer, you can always wait for your favorite movie to come on video. These simple techniques can usually save you considerable money in your budget.

Another item in your budget could be the cost of prescription medicines and drugs. If you don't have a prescription plan, the cost of medication can be staggering. Lamisil, which is used to treat certain types of nail fungus, costs over $200 for a one-month supply. To help defray the cost of medication, all drugstores can offer you generic forms of medication instead of name brands. They are usually just as good and cost much less.

Your doctor can also be a source of savings. Many doctors or almost all of them are involved with salespersons who give them free samples of medications to recommend to their patients. Oftentimes you can get these samples for nothing because that is why they are there, for you to try. It is always a good idea to ask your doctor for samples of medications that they are recommending. This can save you a few dollars.

In every budget, you should always set aside money for savings, college funds, and retirement. It is estimated that you will need $200,000 at retirement to withdraw about $1,350 per month for twenty years. The cost of college is averaging about $200,000 per year, and you need to set up a college fund at the birth of each child to account for this cost.

A savings plan is a must. You should save a minimum of 10 percent of your income per month to account for those rainy days because, believe me, it will rain. You could suddenly get sick and be unable to work for a period of time, and you need a ready supply of cash that can sustain your lifestyle for at least six to twelve months. Therefore when you are building certain items into your budget, don't ever leave out a savings plan. You can eliminate a lot of other things, but a savings plan taking into consideration a rainy day, college, and retirement funds are absolutely necessary in any budget.

Using the table I referred to earlier, break up your net income into monthly amounts and then determine the monthly cost of each item listed in the budget example. Then insert those amounts in the table. Keep a record of every expenditure that you make for the listed item. Do this for several months to determine a pattern and insert these amounts in the "spent" column.

Add the totals in each column to determine if your "spent column" is greater than your "budgeted column." If it is, then you have a serious problem. Go through each item to determine what can be eliminated or reduced and take appropriate action, remembering not to reduce savings if possible. Unfortunately you cannot eliminate the essentials like food, shelter, and utilities. If you continue to monitor your budget on a monthly basis, you will find a sense of order will come into your life and life will become much easier. This module is intended as a guide and not meant to substitute sound financial judgment.

How to Stop Smoking Cigarettes

The abuse of drugs is perhaps one of the worst problems that we face in society. It is my belief that drug abuse starts with cigarettes. In fact, some of the large cigarette manufacturers are now admitting that smoking cigarettes can become addictive. The key ingredient in cigarettes is nicotine, a substance so highly addictive that a pack of cigarettes carry a warning label attesting to the dangers of smoking. You would think that people would seriously consider this warning and quit smoking cigarettes, but smoking is so addictive that people would rather die from lung cancer than quit.

Is this a serious problem or not? Why would you rather die than give up cigarettes? The reason is that most people can't stop because of the hold that smoking has on the body and mind. Many books have been written with various cures, but cigarette smoking continues to rise almost daily. Children as young as nine and ten years old are already hooked on cigarettes, beginning their death march at such a young age. "How can we stop this vicious cycle?" is the question that nobody appears able to answer. In this module, I will join the ranks of another person trying to stop the slow march to an early death from lung cancer.

I remember starting my death march at seventeen. Slowly year after year, I continued my death march until I was about thirty-seven before I realized I had destroyed my health from asthma and emphysema. During those twenty years, I tried to stop many times, but I got the shakes so bad that each time I stopped for a week, I went back to smoking. Now when I look back and remember that a pack of Winston cost fifty-five cents and they cost some places more than five dollars today, I shudder at the amount of money that I would have thrown away to keep me on my slow march to death from emphysema and lung cancer.

The only reason I was able to quit is because I got pneumonia and every time I tried to smoke a cigarette, the pain was so excruciating that even my toes were hurting. I knew then that I had to quit smoking or die, and just like that, I decided that life was a little bit better than dying. I just quit, which brings us to the very best method for quitting smoking cigarettes, to just quit "cold turkey." Unless you get pneumonia and your toes are hurting, this method is very hard to do, but it is the most effective. Mind over matter is all it takes.

Let us examine the method of cold turkey for quitting cigarettes. The key thing with this method is dealing with the pain and suffering and figuring out what to do with your hands. When you quit, you will find yourself constantly bringing your hands up to your mouth, especially after meals and while having a drink. It is just a reflex action. If you do something long enough, your mind will tell your body to just do it, like classical conditioning.

Nicotine is a drug, and it works on the pleasure principle. Smoking a cigarette is enjoyable. It makes you feel good. It gives you energy and relaxes your mind and body. If you mix a cigarette with a drink, it is even more enjoyable. Most smokers can sit at a bar for hours and drink, smoke, and talk for hours because it is enjoyable, mainly because the chemical compounds in alcohol and tobacco work on the pleasure principle of the brain. It is like receiving a surge or a spark, causing a sensation of euphoria. It is almost as good as making love without having a partner.

Why would a person want to stop such a feeling and substitute it with the pain and suffering from not having a cigarette? In fact, it is almost impossible to do unless you have a plan of attack to substitute for the pain and suffering that you will experience while trying to quit smoking cigarettes. You see, pain and suffering come in two forms: physical and psychological pain. You can reduce both by substituting something that is pleasurable and healthy. Several things come to mind, like dieting and exercising, listening to music, daydreaming, taking a walk, writing poems or letters, and so on. You cannot stop smoking unless you can change your mind-set by substituting something else for you to do other than raiding the refrigerator.

The principle of substitution is extremely important during the first two to three days of your cold turkey. Without this plan of attack, you will certainly fail and continue on your slow march to death from lung cancer, throat cancer, or some other cessation of life, like a stroke or heart attack. You can reduce the problem of not knowing what to do with your hands by keeping a pen and paper nearby, and every time you begin to raise your hand to your mouth, grab the pen and begin to write "I don't want a cigarette."

The perfect substitution for quitting cigarettes is exercising. Not only are sit-ups and push-ups an effective substitution, they are a healthy substitution because it starts you on the path of keeping your weight down, which is a major disadvantage of quitting cigarettes. I gained fifty pounds after quitting because for some reason, nicotine acts as an appetite suppressant, and once you quit, the chances are very good that you will put on weight. It is extremely important to immediately begin a program of diet and exercise using low-fat foods, whole-grain cereals, plenty of fresh fruits, green vegetables, nuts, lots and lots of water, and my own special drink of apple cider vinegar water with prune juice and honey. Be careful with the prune juice. Don't go too heavy. Also stay away from pork and all fish that don't have scales and fins, especially lobster, shrimp, and crab. Unfortunately people like all of these things very much, but they are unhealthy because they are scavengers and therefore are unclean. In fact, I like them and have had some difficulties adjusting to not eating them.

As I said earlier, the best and most effective method of quitting smoking cigarettes as well as any drugs is the cold turkey method. The mental and physical pain is the most significant aspect of this method. Although it is an awful price to pay, it only lasts for about a week. If you can get beyond the first week, you are home free, especially if you are able to change your mind-set using the principles of substitution to ward off the physical and psychological abuse.

The last and least effective method for quitting smoking cigarettes is based on a gradual process. If I had 1 percent of the money that has been made using this method, my children and my children's children would be set for life. The folks who created the patch, nicotine gum, and a host of other remedies for quitting smoking are rich to no end. They don't want you to quit smoking. They want you to remain hooked on nicotine so they can continue to reap huge profits. Who the hell cares if you continue your slow march to death from lung cancer or some other life-threatening disease by continuing to smoke cigarettes?

In fact, I am working on one of these gradual methods for you to quit smoking. I am calling it the "not" pill. It will be intended for you not to stop smoking so I can make a lot of money while you take your slow walk to become a candidate for the boneyard. Regardless of whether you intend to use the "stop at once" approach such as used in the cold turkey method or the gradual method extending over a period of time, you must be willing to stop. Most people don't stop smoking because they don't have the willpower to. They procrastinate, when in actuality, they are not willing to make the sacrifice.

The gradual process is the choice of the folks who are on the journey to quit, but they don't have the commitment level to just quit. These are the folks who use nicotine gum, phony cigarettes, hypnosis, and rationing of cigarettes. These folks rarely quit smoking for more than a few weeks or months and are rarely able to remain smoke free.

Unfortunately, cigarettes are like drugs. Cigarette smokers can't get help until they realize they need help. If they are like I was, they must become very ill before realizing they must quit or die. In fact, some people dying from cancer continue to smoke. The gradual method for quitting cigarettes works for persons who have made up their minds that they will quit, but they need time to get the monkey off their backs.

I am not a proponent of this method because it points toward a weakness in the mental aspect of humans. These folks don't have control over their minds. In order to quit smoking, you must gain control of your mind in spite of the pain and suffering because you know the pain and suffering can't last always. When you can do this, you can quit smoking, drinking, or any other perverse activity that you are involved in.

The gradual method is definitely the less painful of the two basic methods for quitting smoking. It allows you to slowly stop smoking by reducing daily cigarettes from a large quantity to a smaller and smaller quantity over a period of time. It also allows you to put into place an effective method of substitution for cigarettes by using gum, candy, and/or other nicotine-reducing devices. As in any method of quitting smoking, you must be willing to begin a new life using an effective approach to eating and exercising to reduce the effects of the weight gain that are sure to follow from the elimination of cigarettes.

As with anything in life, before you even begin to think about quitting something that is not good for you, you must be willing to pay the price to stop. That price usually requires tremendous sacrifices and a level of commitment far outweighing anything that you have been involved in. Once you are able to ensure yourself in your own mind that you are willing to make this sacrifice, either the "stop at once" method using the technique of cold turkey will work or the gradual method of quitting using the method of an extension over time.

Cigarette smoking as well as any form of tobacco use is extremely harmful for your health, and unless you make the commitment to stop, you will continue on your slow march to death from an incurable disease like cancer. Life is about choices, and the choice is yours either to live or die.

How to Stop Using Drugs

I am in a bottomless pit, and I can't get out. This is an analogy of a junkie. Once you become an addict or a junkie, you find yourself in a pit of ascending and descending stairs always trying to climb out but falling back every day. You wake up every morning, saying "This is the day I am going to stop using drugs." You try very hard, but the pain is too great. Your mind immediately begins to focus on how to get the money to support your habit. By now you have become very creative in finding different ways to get money. You have become a master thief, a superb con man, and an excellent beggar. The only friends you have left now are crack pipes, lines of cocaine, or dirty needles. Your friends, children, and family have long since abandoned you because of your lying and stealing. The only people who know you now are other junkies and the police. You have managed to find yourself in and out of jail. The only consolation is that you have not reached the bottom of the pit. You are still in denial. "I can still quit using drugs" is what you keep telling yourself. You are still able to ascend the stairs even though you descend them more often. What a life!

"I am in a pit, and I can't get out" is the analogy of a junkie. It has been ten years. Once upon a time long ago, you had a promising future. You were a star athlete with everybody wanting to be your friend. They even gave you joints to try and lines of cocaine just to say they got high with you. The adulation went to your head, and before you knew it, ten years had gone by, and the only friend left was the crack pipe. What a life!

In this module, I will attempt to show you several methods for getting off drugs. You must keep in mind that you cannot get off drugs until you are able to admit that you are a junkie. You must also admit that you have a serious sickness and you need help. Unfortunately you can never get help with your sickness until you fall to the bottom of your proverbial pit and truly cannot get out. You must cry out, "I am a junkie!" At this point, you are no longer in denial. So you can see that the first step in getting off drugs is to admit that you are a junkie and need help. When you are able to do this, you are ready to receive help.

Until you reach this point, you will never get out of that pit of ascending and descending stairs because in your mind, you believe you can quit using drugs whenever you want to. Unfortunately this is not true. Once you become a junkie, you no longer have control of your life. Drugs have taken over control of your mind and body. Nothing matters, not mother, father, sister, brother, or even God. Drugs replace everything that used to be important.

Now that you have admitted that you are a junkie, you can proceed to the second step, to get help. When you are doing drugs, help never enters your mind because you never believed that you had a problem. You believed that you could quit whenever you wanted to. Besides you were too busy developing schemes to get money to finance your habit.

If you had looked closely at the times you were in jail, you would have realized that during these periods of incarceration, you either did not use drugs or used them sparingly. During these times, you were forced to not use drugs because you could not get them. This brings me to the first method for getting off drugs, which is the method of deprivation, or cold turkey. This method is probably the hardest but usually the most effective. In this method, the body is starved of drugs. The withdrawal pains are unbearable. Chills and sweats are constant; sleep is nonexistent for perhaps days before the drugs are washed out of the system.

Based on conversations with junkies, it is a like a woman being in intense labor for three or four days with excruciating fevers, chills, and intense pain so severe that you pray to die. You must be strapped down to avoid physical injury. Most former junkies say it is almost impossible to go through this method, but if you are able to do so, it is the most effective method to stop using drugs, especially hard drugs like heroin. This method of cold turkey can be used to stop using any drugs beginning with cigarettes and alcohol and escalating to hard drugs like crack and heroin. This method involves both a physical and mental aspect to it. The physical aspect involves bodily pain; the mental aspect involves the mind. It is always advisable to have an experienced former junkie with a person to keep the person from going crazy.

The second method for getting off drugs is to enroll in a rehab center. This method is only successful when the person truly wants to get off drugs. Counselors who are trained professionals are there to get you through the difficulties. These counselors are often former addicts who know what it takes to get off and stay off drugs. The problem with this method is that most people who enrolled in a rehab center are doing so to please someone else other than themselves.

This usually occurs after a child has been arrested for the first time and they are looking to please the judge in the court system or parents. These folks can't wait until they get out of rehab to hit the pipe again because they are still in denial. In fact, they don't believe they have a problem at all. Folks like these go back and forth into one rehab center after another, usually wasting their rich parents' money. As soon as they get out of rehab, they are calling their supplier to get more drugs and vow to be more careful about getting caught in the future. In their own minds, they are still not junkies. They are truly still in denial.

Rehab centers are the greatest method for getting off drugs once you have reached the bottom of your proverbial pit and cry out "I am a junkie, and I need help." They are staffed to accommodate all of the multifaceted problems encountered by junkies like prostitution, sexual abuse, and parental abuse. In order to be cured of drugs, the root causes of drug usage must be determined. Counselors, doctors, and other professionals are usually on hand to assess the problems and determine a course of action to follow.

The third method for getting off drugs is to change the environment you live in, either by moving away from the neighborhood or disassociating yourself from your former acquaintances. If you return to the same environment, it is much more likely that you will continue to do the same things that you engaged in during the past. In a bankruptcy, you are often looked upon as receiving a fresh start.

The same is true for drugs. Once you have received treatment for a drug problem, you must absolutely change the company you keep or the problem will return very quickly unless your mind has been changed entirely. It is just a matter of time before you try drugs again and your problems will return just as quickly. Enrolling in school is usually a way to change your environment. You will develop new friends with a different focus, usually one that is positive. Developing a new hobby or skill is another way to change your environment.

By the time you reach the stage of being a junkie, the chances are good that you don't have a job. Now is the time to start a new career. Oftentimes once you have an arrest record, it is very difficult for you to get a job. Now may be the perfect time to create your own niche in life by starting a small service-oriented business, like painting, preparing taxes, washing cars, cutting grass, and so on. Just a change in pace could be the perfect solution for getting you off drugs and keeping you clean. You will also notice that some of your old family and friends will be willing to help you now that you have begun to turn your life around.

The fourth and final method for getting off drugs is based on a spiritual encounter. This is perhaps the method that nobody pays any attention to, but it can be the most effective method even more so than cold turkey if you are serious. Getting involved in an organized religion is a surefire method for getting off drugs. Not only will it create a whole new set of values, it will create a whole new set of friends, the most important being a personal relationship with God. The things that you as well as counselors, doctors, and professionals can't do, God can. If you reach out for His help through prayer and sincerity, I am sure that there are numerous times when you are strung out on drugs that you have said, "God, please help me," but as soon as things got a little better, you forgot about God. You see, God not only helps good people, He specializes in helping bad people if they open up their hearts and let Him come in.

Drugs are an all-consuming encounter. The best method for getting off drugs is to never to get on them. Unfortunately, each and every one of us, has probably experimented with drugs of some nature without any noticeable side effects, but many of us have been totally consumed and unable to reach beyond the hold that drugs have on our lives. For those persons, it is important to admit the problem and get help and remember that God Almighty is the total solution for any and all problems.

How to Tell If Your Children
Are Using Drugs

I don't know which is worse in society: welfare, racism, prejudice, or drugs. Each of these plays a significant role in the formation of character in our children and adults alike, but perhaps drugs are worse because of its direct correlation to crime. I would venture to say that 80 percent of the crime committed in this country is directly related to drugs. Think of robberies, shootings, murder, prostitution, auto theft, embezzlement, and any other crime you can think of. It is probably related to drugs of some form or description. I bet if you did a survey of people in prison, a very large percentage have used drugs or continue to use. What these deviants of society are looking for is money to finance their habits.

Almost every country in the world is exposed to drugs of some nature, whether it is alcohol, tobacco, sleeping pills, cocaine, heroin, or marijuana. You see, the problem with drugs is that they alter the capacity of the mind, which causes a person to lose control of their mental abilities. In addition, all drugs have some physical control of a person's body as well, especially alcohol, tobacco, heroin, and cocaine. Drugs are so difficult to stop using because your mind and body become dependent on them because drugs work on the pleasure principle. They make you feel good, and not having them makes you feel bad. Your body and mind become so dependent that you cannot exist without them.

Think of a little thing like coffee. There is a certain small percentage of caffeine in ordinary coffee, and if you drink enough coffee, you will find that it is very difficult to do without it. Your body and mind become dependent on it, and if you do not have a cup of coffee before noon, you will get a headache. Unfortunately, many of us never think of coffee as being a drug, but it is just as addictive as cigarettes.

To become an adult, you must start as a child. What happens when children eight, nine, ten, and eleven years old start using drugs? What kind of a future will they have? Unfortunately, nobody gives a crap until your children are discovered using drugs. In this module, I will attempt to show you a few common methods of how to tell if your children are using drugs.

Let us start with cigarettes. Maybe you don't think that cigarettes are drugs, but unfortunately, they are very much a drug with strong addictive qualities. Nobody pays any attention to the warning label on them, however, because cigarette smoking continues to rise among teenagers and adults. I know tons of people who have tried to stop smoking without success. Everyone I have spoken to says it is too difficult to stop because of the physical and mental stress on the body. They don't care that cigarettes cause serious medical problems.

How can you tell if your child is smoking cigarettes? Perhaps the easiest way to tell is from the smell of their clothing, body, and hair. Cigarettes carry a distinct smell, especially if you are not a smoker. The odor lasts a long time, and it is very easy to detect because it seems to linger much longer on a person's breath, clothing, or hair.

The second thing is money. Cigarettes cost at least two dollars per pack. If your child seems to always need money, ask why. In fact, the easiest way to tell if your child is using cigarettes is to just ask. If you look in a child's eyes, it is very difficult for them to lie without you being able to see it in their eyes. It is very difficult for a liar to look directly at you.

The other thing is the body language. The mouth says one thing, but the body says something totally different. If you look very closely at your child or anyone, the body tells a totally different story than the spoken words.

The third thing is the hiding places for the cigarettes. Where are the usual places that a parent looks for hidden cigarettes? Under the mattress, in pillows, under a shirt, and in pockets. Look for them in the unusual places like shoes and sneakers.

Now let us examine alcohol. Some children start using alcohol as early as the fourth and fifth grades. They start out drinking wine coolers and cheap beer before graduating to cheap wine and then hard liquor. Children start off using celebrations as occasions to drink, things like ballgames, dates, junior and senior proms, graduations, and so on. The first occasion for drinking is usually the first time for getting sick, such as vomiting and hangovers.

As your children enter puberty, watch out for these telltale signs of their first drink. If they get sick enough on that first drink, maybe they won't go beyond this stage, but the chances are good that they will. Unfortunately alcohol, as all other drugs, works on the pleasure principle, and it gives you confidence. Usually you like the way it makes you feel, and once you get by the initial sickness, you begin to like the extra nerves it gives you.

It is important for you as parents to know the telltale signs of early drinking. Your children become a little sassier and much more talkative. Their schoolwork starts to fall off, and they don't want to get up in the mornings. Or if they do get up, they have a headache. Alcohol acts as a depressant, and when you drink too much, you are extra sleepy and sluggish.

The major culprits in encouraging your children to drink are you as parents and their peer groups. You must be concerned about how you drink in front of your children and how much alcohol is around the house. If your children don't see you drinking and there is never any alcohol around the house, the chances are good that your children will not develop a penchant for drinking, especially if you develop a talking relationship with them.

If they feel comfortable talking to you about anything, chances are good that they will not become heavy drinkers. The company a child keeps tells you a lot about them. If you see your child hanging out with undesirables, then you know your child is an undesirable. Start the communication process as soon as possible. They just might be screaming out for attention. Give it to them instead of letting someone else give it to them.

The sense of smell is always a telltale sign of your child developing a drinking problem. If you smell alcohol or tobacco on your child, you must immediately approach the child about the situation, but your approach has to be one of concern and caring instead of chastisement. The best way, as always, to find out about problems with your children is communication. You can learn a lot more by just asking instead of being a detective that is sneaking around. Always keep the door of communication open. Have family meetings at least once every two weeks and always give the child freedom to talk without repercussions. If you use this approach, you will find a lot more honesty and problems can be avoided before it starts.

The key thing with smell is not just the odor of alcohol on the breath and clothes, but the residual effects such as additional use of breath mints, mouthwash, chewing gum, and eye drops for those red eyes. If you notice an increase in the use of these products, look out. If you keep liquor around the house and you gradually start to notice that a little bit is missing, proceed with due haste to thrash out the problems because by now you really have a problem. Never tiptoe around the problem. Assume the worst and get help.

Marijuana is like a graduation. You have gone from a novice to the big time. By now you have learned to drink either beer, wine, liquor, or all of the above. You now have decided to try your first joint. It is usually given to you by one of your peer group. Unless you have also started to smoke cigarettes, you will not notice any distinguishable differences at first because you don't know how to inhale. Once you begin to practice, usually with friends, you learn to inhale, and bingo, you are really in the big time. The euphoria is intense. Your head spins wildly. You feel giddy and good. Your sense of communication is heightening. Your confidence is exhilarating. Man, you feel good, like nothing you have ever experienced. The pleasure principle is at the top of its game.

Little do you know, this is the start of a catastrophe. In the beginning, there does not appear to be a problem. You wake up in the mornings without a headache, feeling refreshed and happy with the world. You think marijuana is the greatest thing in the world. Nobody could even begin to make you believe that it is the beginning of the road to harder drugs like cocaine, crack, and heroin. You say, "This could never happen to me."

In actuality, it very well could take a long time, but eventually you will try cocaine or maybe crack cocaine and even heroin. Once you take that first hit, you are truly on your way to the ultimate destruction, that of an addict or a junkie. Drugs can consume your every existence. You live not for life but for drugs. Nothing else matters, not family, friends, children, or whatever. The only thing that matters is money for drugs. You will stoop to the lowest level of existence to get the money for drugs. Usually you end up dead or in jail. Don't do it. With every fiber of your body, you should stay away from drugs.

As parents, how can we tell when our children are using marijuana? Well, the very first thing as always is to ask them and watch their friends. Once you get beyond this, you should check for the unusual smell of marijuana. It has a peculiar smell that is easy to recognize on a person's body, clothing, and hair. A person's fingers and nails become discolored with a brownish tint. Little seeds are found in the car and in and around the house. Small burn holes appear on the car seats and on a person's clothing. Eyes are always watery, glassy, and red. Lips and mouth are constantly dry, and a person is always thirsty and hungry, usually for sweets. Also suddenly notice use of eye drops. Chewing gum and breath mints become favorite products for their use. If you notice any of these telltale signs, then you have a serious problem. Take remedial steps immediately. At this point, there is still hope before cocaine and other harder drugs are involved.

If your child gets beyond marijuana and ventures into cocaine, crack, and/or heroin, your and their problems are now in full bloom. Money now becomes the central issue. Things suddenly start to disappear. School becomes nonexistent. They are now at the point of needing money to finance their habits. Strange characters, cars, and people start to visit more often. Whispers start to circulate, appearances begin to change, and a constant irritability is always present. Within a short time, the police start to circle your block, and shortly thereafter, your child is arrested for stealing. Your life and theirs will never be the same. Drugs will now consume both.

Before total consumption, it is important for you as parents to be able to recognize the early warning signs of drug usage, starting with cigarettes. Don't take cigarettes so lightly. It is the very first warning sign of a bigger problem. Always remember that the easiest way to find out what is happening with your children is to just ask. Believe it or not, they want you to ask. It shows that you care. Your life should never be so busy that you cannot spend time with them. Just this alone will help you to help them. Remember to find out what is happening with your children. Just ask.

How to Treat Your Woman Right

What is the difference between having a woman or girlfriend and having a wife? In actuality, very little is different except perhaps with a wife there is a written contract. The written contract is a binding legal agreement and, once breached, allows the wife an opportunity to file for divorce to rescind the contract and receive some type of settlement. A girlfriend or your woman ordinarily does not have this right except in certain states that recognize common-law marriages.

As a man, whether you have a girlfriend, a wife, or a woman, as some folks like to describe their significant other, you should treat them with as much respect as you would treat yourself or your mother. In this module, I will attempt to show you how to treat your woman right regardless of how the situation is classified. They are one and the same.

In fact, if you do not treat her with the respect that you accord yourself or your mother, it is my opinion that you are not a man. A pimp, in my opinion, is less than a man because he uses women to satisfy his own selfish motives and gains a monetary value from exploiting them. His deeds are dastardly and degrading not only to the women who serve him but to all women in general. A man who thinks like a pimp is less than a man. Now that we have established a thought process, let us proceed on how to treat your woman right.

The number-one thing in treating your woman right is to stay away from the violence aspect of a relationship. Unfortunately, the world is full of violence in its own rights, and violence toward someone you profess to love is a travesty. How can you love someone and commit atrocious acts of violence? Only a sick mind can perceive such an act of cowardice. A woman was created to be a beautiful helpmate for man. How can she be beautiful and willing to help you when she is bloodied and bruised? A man who stoops to this level of cruelty has a sick mind and needs help with his mental stability.

Classical conditioning through beatings and rewards may work for a dog, but it should never be considered for your woman. If she needs to be controlled from that perspective, she needs to be encouraged to seek counseling in her own rights. The battered women syndrome is already quite prevalent in society and does not need additional candidates to further its cause. A good man would never under any circumstances commit acts of violence toward his woman. If his thought process is prone toward violence to someone he professes to love, he needs a change of venue. This can be done through counseling and enrollment in a gym where he can beat the crap out of a boxing bag.

The number-two thing in how to treat your woman right is the avoidance of the degradation of women. Although I love all kinds of music, including rap, I have found that many aspects of rap music is degrading to women. It treats them as sex objects to be used for sexual exploitation through abnormal sexual acts. I know that the artists and the music industry will say that rap music is just an expression of humankind's creativity and has no relevant correlation to society, but I believe that this is definitely not true. I believe that the sex, violence, profanity, and lewd name-calling create a subculture of misfits, maybe not from the artists creating the music but certainly from the children who are exposed to it.

Over the years, I have had the opportunity to be around children in projects and daycare centers, and much of their mannerisms and conversation is explicit in its manifestation of rap music. I see a weakening of morality in small children who are acting out the lyrics of much of the present-day rap music. Small children as little as four years old are cursing and dancing sexually suggestively as they listen to rap artists degrade and abuse women. I see little girls backing their ass up to little boys who are rocking on them. It is not a pleasant thing to hear and see some of the things that are happening at such a young and impressionable age.

The sexual revolution has created young men encouraging and, in some cases, forcing women to perform all kinds of abnormal sexual acts to remain their women. I believe that this degradation of your woman is definitely not the way to pursue how to treat your woman right. A woman was created as a special, beautiful creature not to be sexually, physically, and mentally abused to satisfy a man's fantasy or hers, for that matter.

The number-three criteria in how to treat your woman right is to take responsibility for your actions regarding children resulting from a relationship, whether it is your children or someone else's. A man should never allow a child to question, "Who is my father? Where is my father?" If you lay down with a woman enough to father a child, there should be no question that you will be responsible for that child. That child should never have to become a ward of society on the welfare rolls and left to be raised in the streets without the guidance of a loving father. The court system should never force you to pay child support.

If you fathered a child, whether it is a mistake or not, you should be willing to accept the responsibilities for helping to raise that child. In fact, when you lay down with a woman, there is always the possibility that something could happen, either a baby or disease. I don't believe in safe sex for men and women. I believe in no sex for men and women unless you are married. Safe sex is good, but abstinence is better until marriage. I believe that when boys and girls are ready for sex, they should be ready for marriage. If you do the crime, then you must do the time and pay the fine.

The matter of children being involved that are not yours should be addressed at the beginning of a relationship. Oftentimes a woman makes a mistake and has a child or even more than one and is left holding the bag without the benefit of a caring person to help her with the children. If you get involved in a relationship like this, the children should not be made to suffer. You should be concerned enough about the children's plight before beginning such a relationship. A man who is treating his woman right is willing to help in such a relationship if he becomes involved with her.

I am not advocating adoption, but a man involved in a relationship with other children should be responsible enough to do what he can to help the situation even though they are not his. A child needs guidance from a good person more so than a lack of guidance from the child's father. Sometimes it is very difficult to deal with someone else's children, but it is often necessary if you want a relationship with the woman.

There are many men who marry women with children from a previous affair, but it is not easy to do because very few men want a ready-made family. It takes a real man to deal with such a relationship. I imagine, this is, why so many women with children have difficulties getting married and end up having more children from another man who is not responsible.

The final criteria for knowing how to treat your woman right is to know how to please her emotionally and sexually. Although I am not a proponent of sex before marriage for either a man or woman, I believe it is important to know how to satisfy your woman to keep her happy. Satisfying her starts with respect. Every woman wants to be loved and appreciated. Compliment her when she looks good, and never ever take her for granted. Buy her some flowers every now and then and do it on some special occasions like her birthday. Women go crazy when you have flowers sent to her job. She becomes the envy of all the other women on her job. This makes her feel very special. Women are emotional. Flowers make them feel loved and appreciated.

I read in a book written by Nauru Hayden that I am quoting directly from, which states,

- "I believe in marriage. I also believe in faithfulness in marriage … I believe god gave us our sex organs to bond us together in pleasure within our marriage. And through this incredible pleasure, to keep us faithful to each other as long as we both shall live."
- "Most women are faking orgasms and are deeply dissatisfied sexually with their husbands and their marriages and are looking for 'Mr. right' to fulfill them in this very important way."
- "A man will be loved as never before when he is able to give his woman the greatest pleasure he can give her—an orgasm, and

when he can do this every time they make love, her love will know no bounds."

When we examine this quotation, the key thing is to know how to give your woman an orgasm. Contrary to popular belief, carrying a big stick and banging her to death is not the way. A woman's body is fragile and sensitive to pain, and banging her to death is painful, especially if you are heavily endowed. I have spoken to many women, and a great majority of them indicate that the actual sex act of intercourse is not the most fulfilling way of making love, especially when you don't know what you are doing. Many of them spoke about the foreplay leading up to the sex act, things like the hugging, kissing, caressing, and lying in each other's arms. Many of them also indicated that the teasing and gentle touches to the clitoris and vaginal area can arouse a woman to an orgasm without even deep penetration with your penis.

What I am saying is that it is very important to communicate with your woman and simply ask her what she likes and practice, practice, practice. Once you have established how to satisfy her sexually and become good at doing it, there is no need for her to stray. In fact, once she begins to achieve an organism, her love will become so undying that there would be no need to look elsewhere. The key ingredient in any relationship is to talk about what makes each other happy and do it over and over again. There is nothing greater than being in love, making love, and having multiple orgasms together.

When we look back on the previous, the things that should jump into your mind on how to treat your woman right is to always treat her with the utmost respect. Cherish her and refrain from degradation using physical, sexual, and mental abuse. Always remain accountable and responsible for your actions toward her, your children, and her children that are not yours. Make sweet love to her every chance you get, and never ever take her for granted.

The Establishment of Christian Schools Under the School Choice Program as It Relates to the Reformation of the Church

s I reflect today, I have come to realize that the world is spiraling out of control and must be brought back into focus through a strong affiliation with God and His Son Jesus as the guiding force in our lives, and it must begin with the church and our school system, which will help to establish laws that will benefit all of humankind. We must take a strong stand against abortions, same-sex marriages, homosexuality, and all forms of sexual deviant behavior, or we will be headed into a Sodom and Gomorrah existence. We must begin this process by a much greater influx of Christian schools to change the fabric of thinking in our communities. I believe school choice is the perfect mechanism for implementing this daunting task, along with the reformation of the church.

The reformation of the church must begin with the reformation of our communities. The so-called ghetto, as evidenced by the living conditions in the black communities, must totally be changed. Education is the way to do it. Our children's way of thinking must be changed from leaving the ghetto to becoming educated so they stay and change the living conditions within the ghetto. Your goal should be to get a good education and reinvest your money within the community by learning to become business owners instead of working for business owners outside our communities. Build your fancy homes in the ghetto and reinvest your money within the ghetto by opening businesses and employing the members of your community to run and operate these businesses.

Very successful people like athletes and entertainers must stop leaving our communities to build some big house in the so-called white community and reinvest their riches in the neighborhoods they grew up in. As money is reinvested in the ghetto, the ghetto will take on a new look and eventually cease to be classified as a ghetto. Housing and business conditions will change for the better, and the stigma of the ghetto will no longer exist.

The first thing that must be done is to change the thinking in our black communities by shutting down the abundance of liquor stores and eliminating drug sales in the black communities. The second thing that must be changed is the negative impact of our music on our children from women being classified as bitches, whores, and sex objects and men being classified as niggers and studs. Our mode of dress must be changed from baggy clothes hanging off our exteriors exposing our underwear and tattoos all over our bodies. These things are the main source of mind control in our communities and must be dealt with to stymie the escalating lack of morality in our culture. Much too much time, effort, and energy are spent dealing with alcohol and drug use in our communities, causing our families to suffer because our men are increasingly dependent on these items without realizing the true effect on our and our children's behavior.

Fathers are missing in action or languishing in some morbid state of inaction, not providing the nurturing our children need to adjust to an ever-changing and demanding society. Fathers must become fathers and not just men who went half on a baby.

A spiritual revolution is necessary to change the course of history, and it must be ushered in by the church taking control of the education of our children. We must get back to a new beginning, which is the ending of the world as was known when Christ ascended into heaven and left the world on the right course to salvation through Jesus and

His disciples. The church has since wavered due to the modification of the church and the Christianity entrusted to Christ's disciples and His followers.

The church was successfully modified when the pope was installed as the head of the Roman Catholic Church. Jesus Christ was no longer the central figure in this new religion that He had formed and continued by His twelve disciples and followers after He ascended into heaven and left His disciples specific instructions to go into all the world and make disciples of all nations, baptizing them in the name of the Father, the Son, and the Holy Spirit and teaching them to obey everything He has commanded you. "And surely I am with always, to the very end of the age" (see Matthew 28:16–20 KJV) and further expressed by Mark 16:15–20 KJV, which states, "Go into all the world and preach the good news to all creation. Whoever believes and is baptized will be saved, but whosoever does not believe will be condemned. And these signs will accompany those who believe."

In Jesus's name, they shall drive out demons. They shall speak in new tongues. They shall pick up snakes with their hands, and when they drink deadly poison, it shall not hurt them at all. They shall place their hands on sick people, and they shall get well. After the Lord Jesus had spoken to them, He was taken up to heaven, and He sat at the right hand of God. "Then the disciples went out and preached everywhere, and the Lord worked with them and confirmed His words with the signs that accompanied it."

The church spread like a California wildfire and threatened the very existence of the Roman Empire, causing the Roman government to devise means of controlling it through persecutions of Christians and all other types of cruel and inhumane treatment. This only made the church stronger, and Rome began to infiltrate the church and finally convinced the Church to "water down" or "tone down their fervent pursuit of following this man called Jesus that had been crucified." The battle of the church versus the state or government had truly begun. The church was winning big, and Rome began to step up measures to control it, successfully ending with the creation of Catholicism with a man called a "pope" and a woman called the "Virgin Mary" being created to represent the central authority in the church instead of "Jesus the Christ."

From that point on until the present time, the church has lost its flavor. Humankind's law has almost replaced God's law so that things like abortions, homosexuality, same-sex marriages, mercy killings, and all other social deviant behaviors have become almost accepted or at least tolerated for the sake of not violating humankind's rights when the question should be "What about God's rights?"

Unless the church is reformed to become the church that Jesus founded when He said "Upon this rock, I will build my church," which means "Jesus Church," we as a people are heading headlong into condemnation so eloquently expressed by Mark 16:15–18, which states those who believe and are baptized will be saved and whosoever does not believe will be condemned.

Condemnation is all around us as we face violence of all types and descriptions, rampant drug use, teachers and students having sex, gangs controlling our streets and neighborhoods, churches turning a deaf ear, schools crumbling due to serious disciplinary problems, overcrowded classrooms, and so forth. Serious changes are necessary, and it must begin with the church taking control of our communities by becoming the central source of educating our children through the establishment of Christian schools.

In the state of South Carolina and many other large states, almost seven out of ten black kids drop out of school before graduating from high school. In other words, only three out of ten black kids are obtaining a high school diploma. What are the fates of these seven out of ten kids? They are headed to jail from selling drugs, breaking into our homes, robbing banks, or heading to the graveyard much too early for an uneventful life. They are destined to become wards of society through welfare and other forms of governmental handouts.

Our public schools in the black communities are failing to properly educate our children because our children are forced to attend crumbling schools in these communities without a choice of attending other schools because of laws requiring students to attend schools in their own so-called districts. We must take control of these staggering consequences or face the reality of a world crumbling from decadence. Sodom and Gomorrah will surely be revisited. How can we do it? I can only see it happening with a total spiritual revolution headed by the church to change the moral fabric of our young men and women.

The reformation of the world must begin with the reformation of the church. The church must become the focal point for changing our communities by the establishment of Christian schools to change the value system of our communities. Christian schools can be established by private donations or using existing infrastructures already in existence, things like family life centers, church classrooms, and so on.

Christian schools are not a new phenomenon. They have been in existence forever, starting with Catholic schools. Many parents who could afford it sent their children to Catholic schools because it was well known that these children received a better education enhanced by the spiritual perspective that was present in the schools. The teachers, administrators, and so forth were Christians, which helped to instill a strong moral value in the children. In fact when I was coming up as a child, many churches had their own elementary schools, and the quality of education and the character of the children were simply better. A prime example of a good Christian school in today's world is V.V. Reid Elementary School under the auspices of Reid Chapel AME Church in Columbia, South Carolina, which produces outstanding students far advanced over their public school counterparts with zero discipline problems.

The ideal solution for the establishment of Christian schools, however, is by using a government program already in place called School Choice, which is working great in places like Milwaukee, Wisconsin, and several other states and cities using charter schools and various voucher programs. The church is Jesus's bride, and He is coming back to claim it without a spot or a blemish. The church and the government must be reformed to allow this to happen.

Where do we begin? We must begin with the community. The church must take control of the community by becoming totally involved in the education of our children. Religious studies must be the first course taught in our schools. Prayer, praise, and worship must become the core curriculum. Every large church or group of smaller churches must establish Christian schools to reshape the thinking of our children from the way of the world to the way of God. The church and the community must petition our lawmakers to institute a School Choice program that is working so great in Milwaukee so the $12,000 to $15,000 per year spent on each student in public schools can be allocated to parents and students within the so-called ghetto to allow communities to open their own schools and educate our children to ensure that truly no child is left behind.

The church must be at the forefront of this movement and concentrate on building Christian schools to change the thinking of our children to ward off the failure of our public schools to educate our children so that seven out of ten children in the black community fail to graduate from high schools in the state of South Carolina and many other states as well.

School Choice is the way of the future and is an excellent tool to change the quality of education and the moral fiber of our children to ensure that no child is truly left behind. School Choice works because it frees up $12,000 to $15,000 per year per child to be used to build Christian schools within our communities or, at worst, obtain a voucher to travel to a school of your choice if you provide for your own transportation.

The educational system, as it exists in almost all states, only allows a child to attend a school within their own district, thereby ensuring a perpetuation of very bad schools in the black community based mostly on economics and children not at least obtaining a high school diploma to obtain at least a halfway decent job. Schools and churches are perhaps the two most segregated institutions in the world. Black kids go to black schools; white kids go to white schools.

Check churches. They are the same. In mixed neighborhoods, there is a greater mixture. Integration has never truly been accomplished. School Choice would allow a child to go to a better school instead of being forced to attend a failing school in their own community. Seven out of ten black kids not graduating from high school is an alarming statistic and the primary reason for crime and other social disorders in our communities. The church must take control of educating our children through the establishment of Christian schools under the School Choice program that is already law in some cities and states all over the country to change the moral fiber of our communities.

Our elected officials must be held accountable for the failure of our educational system to allow only three out of ten black kids to graduate from high school in South Carolina and many other states as well. Elected officials must be petitioned to pass into law a School Choice program, if we as a people want to change the moral fiber of our communities. The church must be at the forefront of this movement. When this is done, the reformation of the church will begin, and the church will usher in a new beginning.

Proposal to Establish Christian Schools

1. Petition elected officials in South Carolina to pass into law a School Choice program.
2. Build the first Christian school in South Carolina under the School Choice program that is already in place and working great in Milwaukee, Wisconsin.
3. Obtain funds from private contributions and donations from various organizations in addition to the sale of our personal logo line of clothing entitled Gangs for Jesus to finance this endeavor.
4. Recruit students and staff to operate and run this new school in compliance with all course contents and curriculum requirements for various grade levels in the state of South Carolina.
5. Comply with all testing requirements for the state of South Carolina.
6. Institute a monitoring and referral program to ensure that children are maintaining proper academic levels.

Life, Liberty, and the Pursuit of Happiness

L ife, liberty, and the pursuit of happiness are the guiding principles that God bestowed upon all of humankind. We are the only creation of all of God's majesty that has been given this unique quality. When we ponder the magnificence of all of God's creation, we realize that we are indeed the chosen generation. We are able to have life and have it more abundantly. We have been given freedom of choice to elect what we want and what we can become. We can do all of the things that make us happy.

Indeed our forefathers could not fathom the complexities of today's society when they coined this phrase of "life, liberty, and the pursuit of happiness" when the world was at war and thousands of people were dying while trying to gain this unalienable right. God has granted us this right, but humankind constantly tries to take it away. Humankind makes laws that permit abortion, allow capital punishment, and permit same-sex marriages as a reminder that God is no longer at the forefront of our beliefs. Our pursuit of happiness is relegated to the vices of the world and how these vices cause contentment instead of happiness.

Let us examine life. What is it, or when does it begin? When does it end, and who is responsible for ending it? We need to examine this from two perspectives, that is, from God's versus humankind's. We need to know that they are vastly different. Do you think that abortions are humankind's or God's perspective? What about capital punishment, mercy killing, and suicide? Are they God's or humankind's perspective? What about same sex-arrangements and marriages? Are they God's or humankind's perspective? What about sexual deviant behavior like oral sex, adultery, and fornication? Are they man-made, or are they God-related?

Anyone in their right mind would know that these aspects of how we live in society are vastly different from how God expects us to live. In other words, humankind's way of life is directly opposite of what God expects of us. "For God so love the world that he gave his only begotten son and whosoever believes in him should not perish but have everlasting life" (John 3:16). "Man's way of life will lead to death but God's way will lead to everlasting life." Proverb 9:35–36 states, "For whosoever finds me finds life, and shall obtain favor of the Lord. But he that sins against me wrong his own soul."

All those who hate the Lord love death. So the key to life is to love God and live a sin-free life. That can only be done when we give our life to Christ and follow His teachings. In fact, if we give our life to Christ and follow His teachings, things like abortions, same-sex marriages, capital punishment, and mercy killings would never be allowed in our society. We would know that these things are tools of the devil and enemies of God. We must understand that only God has control over life. He decides whether we live or die and under what circumstances, but humankind can hasten death through sin, for it is said that "he that sin against me wrong his own soul and all those that hate me love death."

Why are things like abortions, capital punishment, mercy killings, and same-sex marriages enemies of God? The number-one reason is that God states "thou shall not kill." He did specify that we can kill for various reasons. It states that thou shall not kill, period. Even wars are killing and would never occur if the world followed Jesus's teachings. In fact, it is said that the world would be at such total peace that a child could play in a den of rattlesnakes and would not be harmed.

The second thing that God said to humankind is to be fruitful and multiply. And how is multiplication done? Genesis 4:1 KJV states, "Adam knew his wife; and she conceived, and bared Cain, and said, I have gotten a man from the Lord." The key thing is this: Adam knew his wife, and she conceived and received a human from God. Therefore, it is God's intentions for man and wife to have sex and conceive. That is the perfect will of God, and anything different from that is contrary to His perfect will.

I am not saying that God will not permit conception other than between a man and his wife, but only that it is His will that life is conceived this way. Humankind's perspective of creating life is by any means possible, and it is therefore against the will of God and a sin against Him. The commission of the act is a sin, but God has the power to determine if life is conceived. In fact, all life is conceived between a male and a female, not two males or two females. Therefore, same-sex arrangements are human products and not sanctioned by God. It is a sin and will lead to death.

Laws should never ever be created to serve the whims of humans when they are contrary to God's will. Things like abortions, capital punishments, mercy killings, and same-sex marriages should never ever be permitted because they are contrary to God's will and are not sanctioned by God but sanctioned by humankind. Only God has the power to create life by the unity of a man and his wife, which is the perfect will of God or by a man and another woman under a sinful relationship. Things like test-tube babies, artificial insemination, and cloning are man-made creations that are enemies of God and should not be passed into law. The government should be governed by God's laws and create laws that strictly adhere to the Ten Commandments and the Beatitudes as taught by Jesus in his Sermon on the Mount. When such occurs, we will have life and have it more abundantly.

When we as a people are able to live life under purely God's direction, we will be liberated from all fears, anxieties, and concerns about the conditions of the world. There will be such total peace that a child could play in the den of rattlesnakes without any fear. There will be no need for wars, hatred, or killings. At that time, we will be totally liberated from the cares of the world, and true happiness can usher itself into our hearts. Psalm 128 KJV says it best,

Blessed is every one that fears the Lord and walk in his ways. For they shall eat from the labor of their hands, happy shall they be and it shall be well with them. Their wife shall be as a fruitful vine by the side of their house and their children like olive plants around their table. Oh what pure happiness that will be. In our lifetime perhaps never, but that day will come when Jesus returns.

Qualities of People Chosen by God

1. Holiness: to be set apart and separate. We are to be separated from everything that stains and dirties our lives. We are free of all sinful thoughts, destructive emotions, unclean images, impure motives, and questionable activities. For a biblical reference, go to Isaiah 35:8.
2. Pure in heart: to be singular in substance without any imperfections or impurities. "Blessed are the pure in heart for they shall see god" (Matthew 5:8 KJV). See also Matthew 10:37–39.
3. Contrite in heart: to be humble and repentant before God. Read Luke 15:11–32 regarding the prodigal son. Also read Psalm 34:18 and 51:1–17 to gain more insight into what is meant by a contrite heart.
4. Fear of God: fear brings a sense of awe, respect, and reverence toward God and His wrath. Often, we are more fearful of other humans than God. Jesus said in Matthew 10:28 KJV, "Do not be afraid of those who kill the body. Rather be afraid of the one who can destroy both the body and the soul."
5. Faithfulness: steadfast, dedicated, dependable, and worthy of trust. "Be faithful even to the point of death and I will give you the crown of life" (Revelation 2:10). God is searching for men He can trust to intercede on behalf of our nation. Read Ezekiel 22:30.

6. Obedience: our obedience to Christ is proof to others that we are indeed saved and just not saying it with words but showing it with our actions. Read 1 Samuel 15:22 and 1 John 5:3.

7. Actively seek and love God: "seek with all your heart and all your might, and you shall find god" (Jeremiah 29:11–12 KJV). We love God because He first loves us. Can you love God and hate your brother? Read 1 John 4:19–21 KJV.

8. Actively become a servant of God. Whatever you do, work at it with all your heart as if you are working for the Lord as a reward, for great is your reward in heaven. Remember, you can only serve one master, so let that master be God instead of humankind. Read (Colossians 3:23–24 KJV). And(Romans 8:28 KJV).

9. All of my biblical quotations are taken from the King James Version.

Repent and Live or Stay Wicked and Die

There are five steps to salvation: hear the word of God, believe the word of God, repent of your sins, confess Christ as your Savior, and be baptized for the remission of your sins and receive the Holy Ghost. Perhaps the hardest part of reaching salvation is to repent of your sins. If you can repent, you will live or stay wicked, and you will die.

Let's look at (Ezekiel 18:20–32 KJV).

> the soul that sinneth, it shall die. The son shall not bear the iniquity of the father, neither the father bear the iniquity of the son. The righteousness of the righteous shall be upon him, and the wickedness of the wicked shall be upon him. In other word everyone is in control of its own destiny. But if the wicked will turn from all his sins that he hath committed, and keep all my statues, and do that which is lawful and right, he shall surely live, he shall not die.

In other words, if you repent and turn away from your evil ways, you will live in God's kingdom. It goes on to say that all the transgressions that the wicked had committed, they shall not be mentioned unto Him:

in the righteousness that they had done, they shall live. In other words, if you repent, you will be saved.

Now let us look at the person who is already considered righteous. When the righteous turn away from their righteousness and commit iniquity and doeth according to all the abominations that the wicked person do, shall they live? The answer is no. All the righteousness they had done shall not be mentioned. In the trespasses that they trespassed and in the sins that they sinned; in them shall they die.

In other words, when you are righteous and fall, that is, someone like a preacher or your prior righteousness cannot save you. You will be judged based on your fall from grace or wickedness. It continues to say that when a righteous person turns away from their righteousness and commits iniquity and dies in them, it is for the iniquity that they had done shall they die. In other words, God always gives you a chance to repent and be saved or remain wicked and die.

In fact, God takes no pleasure in death. He would much rather you change from your wicked ways and live. This act of changing is the act of repentance. God takes great pleasure in the wicked repenting and turning away from his evil ways. In fact, when the wicked turn away from the wickedness they had committed and do what is lawful and right, they shall save their soul alive. In other words, salvation comes from repenting. "Therefore I will judge you o house of Israel, every one according to his ways, saith the Lord God. Repent and turn yourselves from all your transgressions; so iniquity shall not be your ruin."

In other words, if you do not repent, you will be consumed and/or die. God takes pleasure in us repenting and turning to Him for our salvation, for He said, "I have no pleasure in the death of him that dieth, saith the Lord God: wherefore turn yourselves and live."

The wicked cannot enter the kingdom of God. Only the pure in heart shall see God. Therefore it becomes a complete necessity that we change from the ways of the world to be saved and enter the kingdom of heaven or remain wicked and go to eternal damnation. I say to you, my dear brothers, repent and be saved or remain wicked and die.

God Has the Power to Do What Humankind Cannot Do

Genesis 1–26 states that God made humankind in our image after His likeness and gave us dominion over the fish of the sea, the fowls of the air, the cattle, and all the earth and every creeping thing that creepeth upon the earth. In essence, humankind has the power over all the earth and control over the beast of the sea and all animals. In fact, humankind was created to be like God to be perfect, but unfortunately we failed in His pursuit of perfection because of sin.

The first sin entered the world because of disobedience when humankind disobeyed God by eating from the fruit of the Tree of Knowledge of Good and Evil. This sin created a separation from God and caused humankind's imperfection and humankind to be less powerful than God is. Humans can do almost anything, but God has the power to do what we cannot do. In fact, there is nothing that God cannot do. He has the power to create, destroy, change things, raise the dead, heal the sick, or make the lame to walk. He has the power to sustain life or take away life at any time that He wants.

Let's look at Leviticus 10:1–2 and 16:12 KJV. Two priests, Nadab and Abihu, sons of Aaron, Moses' brother, were given instructions on how to burn incense, and when they decided that they could improve on God's instructions and do things their way, a bolt of fire shot from heaven and killed both of them instantly. When God tells you to do something one way, it is very wise to do what God says, or you just might be consumed. Even when humankind says no, God can say yes. There is nothing too hard for God. He has total power, not humankind's power, but God's power.

Now let us examine Moses. But before we do so, we need to understand why Moses was so significant in God's display of power over humankind. You see, Moses had doubt about his own ability. Although God chose him to rescue the children of Israel from their bondage in Egypt, he did not believe that he could accomplish the job.

Let's look at Exodus 3, beginning with verse 7, and the Lord said, "Surely I have seen the affliction of my people which are in Egypt and heard their cry by reason of their taskmasters; for I know their sorrows." God went on to say in verse 10, "Come now therefore, and I will send thee unto Pharaoh that thou may bring forth my people, the children of Israel, out of Egypt and Moses said unto God, Who am I, that I should go unto Pharaoh and that I should bring forth the children of Israel out of Egypt?"

You see, Moses had doubt about his ability even after God told him what to do. He asked, "Who am I that I should go to Pharaoh?" You see, Pharaoh was the most powerful man on the face of the earth, and Moses did not believe that he could do the job, but God was saying to Moses, "He is only a man, and I am God, and even the great Pharaoh cannot stand up to me." God has the power to do what humankind cannot do. Moses went on to say in Exodus 4:10 KJV,

> O my Lord, I am not eloquent, neither heretofore, nor since thou has spoken to thy servant for I am slow of speech, and of a slow tongue and the Lord said unto him who hath made man's mouth or who maketh the dumb, or deaf, or the seeing or the blind? Have not I the Lord. In all the excuses that man can come up with God is saying to him that there is nothing to hard for God. He can make the dumb to speak the blind to see, and the lame to walk. In fact there is nothing that God cannot do because he made everything and is in control

of everything. God said unto Moses say to the people
I AM THAT I AM, AND THAT I AM SENT YOU.

The bottom line is that God can do what humankind cannot do. You must believe, and everything else falls into place. Jesus is the way, the truth, and the life. No person comes to the Father but by Jesus. Therefore, under all circumstances, try Jesus. The essence of this story is that Moses did not believe that he had the power to accomplish what God had chosen him to do, to rescue God's chosen people from out of Egypt. In fact, he was slow of speech and did not even believe that he could even talk to Pharaoh or convince the Jews that they could leave.,

God told Moses, "I have made you a god to Pharaoh and made Aaron, thy brother, to be your prophet." God equipped Moses with godlike power because He had hardened the heart of Pharaoh to resist Moses so he could show the world the awesome power of God. So even when humankind doesn't believe, God has the power to do what we cannot do.

What Must I Do to Be Saved?

When humankind became separated from God due to sin, we all created a dilemma for ourselves, whether to stay separated or return to God. Ultimately what humankind decides determines their course in life. They must decide to walk in the spirit and not satisfy the lust of the flesh or continue to walk after the flesh.

Unfortunately, humankind tries to do both, which creates the fake Christians we have today, that is, Christians for about two hours on Sunday and non-Christians for the remainder of the time. The flesh lusts toward the things of the world, like adultery, fornication, lust, hatred, and all the pleasures of the world. (See Galatians 5:16) The spirit seeks love, peace, longsuffering, gentleness, goodness, faith, meekness, and temperance.

For about two hours on Sundays, we are all about the spirit, but immediately when church is over or even sometimes during church, our mind is focused on the flesh. Many of us lust after men and women in the church and even after the preacher. When you live in the spirit, you must walk in the spirit. Herein is where the problem lies, living and walking in the spirit. There is a constant battle between the two. It is impossible to inherit the kingdom of God if you live and walk in the flesh, walking after your own pride. The Bible states, "If a man thinks himself to be something when he is nothing, he deceives himself lusting after his own vain glory." Read Galatians 5–6.

To enter the kingdom of heaven, humankind must be saved; therefore, the question becomes: what must I do to be saved? Through God's grace and mercy, we are not consumed. His grace allows God to forgive us for our sins, and His mercy allows Him to help. He is willing to help us and forgive us for our many sins if we would just come to him and ask Him, "What must I do to be saved?" God sent His only begotten Son to show us the way to salvation. His Son, before His ascension to heaven, instructed the twelve apostles what was required. He commissioned them to go into the world and teach all nations, baptizing them in the name of the Father, the Son, and the Holy Ghost, teaching them to observe all things whatsoever they commanded. "And lo, I am with you even unto the end of the world." Those who believe and are baptized shall be saved, and those who believe not shall be dammed.

The disciples were instructed to teach the gospel of Jesus Christ, as they had received it from Him during their three years' journey in His midst. Nobody was better equipped to teach the gospel than His disciples since they had received it firsthand from Him.

The first step in God's plan for humankind's salvation is to hear His words through the gospel of Jesus Christ. Hearing comes from teaching, and who is better to teach than the preacher? Read Romans 10:17 and John 8:32. "He that believeth and is baptized shall be save; he that believeth not shall be damned." See Mark 16:15–16. All Biblical references are taken from the King James Version.

What is belief? It is a persuasion of the mind that something is accepted as truth. It is of the uppermost confidence that something is true without question. We all believe that there is a power greater than we are. We call that power God. The Muslims call that power Allah. "By faith we believe" (Hebrews 11:1 KJV). Faith is the substance of things hoped for, the evidence of things not seen. Without faith, it is impossible to please God, "For he that cometh to God must believe that he is a rewarder of them that diligently seek him."

Therefore, the second part of God's plan for humankind's salvation is to believe. You absolutely must believe that God can do anything but fail. God can never ever fail. He may not come when you want Him, but He is always on time. He is an on-time God. When you are down to your last dime, He comes. Belief is perhaps the easiest. You literally must be stupid if you don't believe in the power of God.

Let's look at Acts 8:37 KJV. "And Philip said if thou believest with all thine heart thou may be baptized. The Eunuch said I believe that Jesus Christ is the Son of God and Philip and the Eunuch went into the water and Philip baptized him."

Philip was the preacher; the Eunuch was a black man from Ethiopia with great authority who handled all the financial affairs for the queen of Ethiopia. In today's vernacular, he would be called the comptroller or the chief financial officer (CFO). I would venture to say that Christianity was introduced in Ethiopia and Africa as well because the news of this baptism spread probably all over Africa. One of Jesus's disciples baptized the queen's Eunuch. Philip was not one of his twelve apostles, but he was one of the first deacons of the early church and, definitely a disciple of Christ. In fact, he was one of the first great preachers and leaders of the early church.

The third step in God's plan for humankind's salvation is to repent. This is perhaps the hardest part of God's plan for humankind's salvation since it works totally against the spirit of God and is in line with the spirit of the world or the spirit of the flesh, the domain of the devil. What is to repent? Repentance is a change of mind-set. It is a feeling of sorrow for some wrongdoing and making a concerted effort not to continue a past behavior.

Jesus teaches in Luke 13:3 KJV that unless you repent, you shall all likewise perish. One of the requirements to get into heaven is that you must become a new creation. Old things are passed away. Nicodemus said it best when he said you must be born again to enter the kingdom of heaven. Men have a problem with repenting because it works against the flesh or the world. The things that give you pleasure are the sins of the world. You absolutely must feel sorry for your sins and repent of them to enter God's kingdom. Changing your mind-set requires a great deal of faith and a total commitment to do God's work, or you will continue to walk after the flesh.

The fourth step in God's plan for humankind's salvation is to confess Christ. Matthew 10:32–33 states, "Whosoever therefore shall confess me before men, him will I confess also before my Father which is in heaven. But whosoever shall deny me before men, him will I also deny before my Father which is in heaven." Romans 10:9–10 states, "If thou shall confess with thy mouth the Lord Jesus Christ. And shall believe in thine heart that God raised him from the dead, Thou shall be saved. For with the heart man believeth unto righteousness; and with the mouth confession is made unto salvation."

In other words, you must be believe in the death, burial, and resurrection of Christ. He died for our sins, was buried for our transgressions, was raised from the dead, and ascended into heaven and sits at the right hand of God Almighty, where he can intercede on behalf of us as sinners.

The fifth and final step in God's plan for humankind's salvation is to be baptized. Peter said on the day of Pentecost in (Acts 2:38) KJV), "Repent and be baptized every one of you in the name of Jesus Christ for the remission of sins and you shall receive the gift of the Holy Ghost." Acts 22:14–16 KJV states that Ananias told Paul that he "had been chosen of God that he should know his will and see the just one and should hear the voice of his mouth for thou shall be a witness unto all men of what thou has seen and heard and why do you delay, arise and be baptized and wash away thy sins calling the name of the Lord."

In other words, the washing away of your sins can only come from baptism. This is God's final step for humankind's salvation. Humankind must be baptized to wash away humankind's sin. Mark 16:16 KJV states, "He that believeth and is baptized shall be saved; but he that believeth not shall be damned."

God's plan for humankind's salvation involves a five-step program. Hear the word of God through the gospel of Jesus Christ. Believe in the gospel. Repent of sins. Confess Christ is the Son of God. And finally, be baptized for the remission of sins and receive the Holy Ghost to keep you in the Spirit of God.

What Are God's Plans
for Humankind?

When God created humankind, He had two very simple instructions for man: have dominion over everything that God had created and do not eat from the Tree of Knowledge of Good and Evil. But humankind disobeyed God's instructions and changed God's plan for humankind. Humankind was no longer like an equal to God because of disobedience. Humankind fell from grace and has been trying to recover ever since. From the moment humankind disobeyed God, they became separated from God because they had attempted to become as wise as God. They had gained the knowledge of good and evil and was now able to have freedom of choices. Unfortunately humankind's choices have been ones that have disagreed with God, but before God decides to totally consume humankind, He continues to give him a second chance to repent.

Humankind constantly refused to do so, and the world became so evil that God had to destroy it through a massive flood that covered the earth. Noah and his family of eight were the only survivors. At that point, God's plans were changed. Noah was told to be fruitful and multiply and replenish the earth, and the Lord said in his heart, "I will not again curse the ground any more for man's sake for the imagination of man's heart is evil from his youth; neither will I, again smite any more every living thing as I had done."

God decided to give humankind a second chance. God blessed Noah and his family and made a covenant with them and their seed not to destroy humankind and everything on the earth in the future. Read Genesis 8–9. God gave Noah and his family a new set of rules, essentially requiring humankind to obey God's commandments to include what to eat for the flesh with the life thereof, which is the "blood thereof shall you not eat and whosoever shed man's blood, by man shall his blood be shed for in the image of God made he man."

God's plans for humankind since the beginning of time have not really changed. They were and still are for us to obey God's instructions and be blessed or disobey and be destroyed. Humankind continued to walk in the way of their own choice, which in their heart is evil, and throughout many generations, God sent prophets to warn humankind to change their evil ways or be destroyed, but humankind consistently refused to do so, and the prophets had no effect.

Finally, God had to send His only begotten Son to show His plans—to return to God and obey His commandments and receive salvation or continue to sin and receive damnation—to us. God's plan through His Son, Jesus, was to spread the gospel of salvation through the Great Commission. The gospel is the good news of Jesus Christ that are centered around three conditions of belief, namely Jesus died on the cross; He was buried in a borrowed tomb, and He was resurrected on the third day and ascended into heaven where He sits at the right hand of God Almighty.

Before His ascension, Jesus told His disciples, "Go ye into all the world, and preach the gospel to every creature. He that believeth and is baptized shall be saved. He that believeth not shall be damned, and these signs shall follow them that believe. In my name shall they cast out devils, they shall speak with new tongues. They shall take up serpents; and if they drink any deadly thing, it shall not hurt them; they shall lay hands on the sick and they shall recover." This account is taken from Mark 16:15–18 KJV.

Matthew 28:18–20 KJV states, "And Jesus came and spoked to them, saying All power is given unto me in heaven and in earth. Go ye therefore and teach all nations, baptizing them in the name of the

Father, and of the Son, and of the Holy Ghost teaching them to observe all things whatsoever I have commanded you and lo, I am with you always even unto the end of the world. Amen."

Therefore, God's plans for humankind is for us to become disciples of Christ and to carry out the Great Commission, spreading the gospel of Jesus Christ throughout all the world and bringing new recruits to God through His Son, Jesus Christ.

The Entrance of Sin into the World

Yielding to temptation brought about the first sin of disobedience of God's commandment when Adam and Eve ate from the Tree of Knowledge of Good and Evil. Jealousy, anger, and premeditation brought about the second sin of murder when Cain killed his brother, Abel. Many other sins have evolved since the beginning of time and will never cease until Jesus returns to establish His kingdom here on earth.

"In the beginning, God created the heavens and the earth"(Genesis 1:1 KJV). From its inception, the earth was void and without form, and darkness covered everything. The Spirit of God moved upon the face of the earth, and God said, "Let there be light and there was light." On the first day, God separated the light from darkness and called the light "day" and the darkness he called "night." On the second day, He created a firmament to divide the waters above from the waters below. The firmament above, He called heaven. On the third day, He created the seas and separated the seas by dry land, which He called earth.

On the fourth day, He created the sun, moon, and stars to divide the days from night and days and weeks into months and seasons. On the fifth day, He created every living creature in the waters in the air and on the ground both male and female. On the sixth day, He made humankind in His likeness and image and gave humankind dominion over everything that was created. Humankind was given dominion over everything from the largest animal to the smallest bird. He made humankind from the dust of the earth and breathed the breath of life into his nostrils, and humankind became a living soul. On the seventh day, God rested and sanctified the seventh day as a day of holiness and completion.

God then planted a garden eastward in Eden and placed a man in this garden. The man's job was to dress and cultivate the garden. The man was given one law or commandment. He was told that he could eat from every tree in the garden except the tree in the middle of the garden called the Tree of Knowledge of Good and Evil. He was told that if he ate from this tree, he would surely die. The first man was called Adam. From the beginning, Adam had no problem with this arrangement. Adam was lonely.

And God decided it was not good for him to live alone so He caused Adam to fall into a deep sleep, removed one of his ribs, and made a woman to be his helpmate. Eve was the name given to her. At that moment, sin was about to creep into the world. The devil in the form of a serpent also lived in the garden, along with all of the other animals that God had created. The serpent was very clever, and he enticed Eve to eat from the tree by telling her that she would not die but would become as wise as God and know the difference between good and evil. Eve gave into temptation and convinced Adam to eat from the tree as well. Once they ate from the tree, they disobeyed God's commandment, creating the very first sin.

Adam and Eve had children. The firstborn was named Cain; the second was named Abel. Cain was a tiller of the soil; Abel was a shepherd. God favored Abel over Cain because Abel gave his first, best, and finest sheep to God as a sacrifice, whereas Cain offered God sacrifices but not necessarily his best and finest crops. Cain became jealous and plotted to kill Abel. He carried out his plan and committed the very first murder. Sin was introduced into the world in its most dreaded form of disobedience of God's commandment not to eat from the Tree of Knowledge of Good and Evil and the murder of one's brother. Am I my brother's keeper?

One man, Adam, introduced sin into the world, and it can only be removed through one man, Jesus Christ. The New Testament is about Jesus Christ. What can wash away our sins? Nothing but the blood of Jesus. Salvation can only be achieved when we accept Jesus as our personal Savior and walk in His light.

The Modification of Christianity

T he day of Pentecost ushered in the era of true Christianity. Read all of Acts 2 KJV to understand the true meaning of Christianity. Some of the key elements are that everyone was on one accord in one place. Everyone was overcome with the Holy Ghost and began to speak with other tongues, as the Spirit gave them utterance. The Holy Ghost felled on all different kinds of people and all nations, not just on the Jews but the Gentiles (non-Jews) as well.

> And it shall come to pass that in the last days I will pour out my spirit upon all flesh: and your sons and daughters shall prophesy and young men shall see visions and old men shall dream dreams and it shall come to pass that that whosoever shall call on the name of the Lord shall be saved.

The main point of Christianity though is the acceptance that Jesus Christ is the only begotten Son of God and that He was sent into the world to suffer and die for our sins. He was buried and raised from the dead on the third day. He ascended into heaven and sits at the right hand of God the Father Almighty, where He shall judge the quick and the dead. And it is only through Him shall we be saved.

All these various nations wanted to know, "What must I do to be saved?" And Peter told them to believe in Jesus Christ, repent of their sins, and be baptized to receive the gift of the Holy Ghost. It went on to say that they continued steadfast in the apostles' doctrine of breaking bread and fellowship through prayer and service to your fellow man. And all who believed were together and had all things in common, sold their possessions and goods, and parted them to all men as every man had need.

In fact, everyone who believed were willing to give up everything and bring it to the church, and the church made up of the twelve apostles and all the other believers were responsible for distributing the proceeds to all men, as they had were shipped from God through His Son Jesus and His apostles to a man called a pope, a symbol called the Virgin Mary, and various other symbols of humankind who were canonized as saints.

A system of idolatry was created, much to the chagrin of God, who states, "Thou shall have no other Gods before me." In essence, the pope and these various symbols could be looked upon as gods. Rome had successfully modified Christianity from Jesus, and the kingdom of God is at hand to a modified form of Christianity. The Roman government controlled the pope and made money from the sale of millions of symbols of the Virgin Mary and various other saints that people wore around their necks. The government, a pope, and a bunch of symbols helped to keep the people under control because a saint was looking after them. This modified form of Christianity still exists even until today through a hundred million forms of denominations, a hundred million forms of religion instead of one universal religion headed by God and His Son, Jesus. The question then becomes: what can the government do to change it, and does the government want to change it?

The Order of Things

How do we know what God's plans are for humankind? Most of us can only speculate, and many of us don't have a clue. We can only know such a complicated answer by how closely we are affiliated with God, through His Son Jesus, who died as a ransom for our sins. With the world spinning out of control from a very bad financial rope called debt that is slowly hanging us, we are slowly hanging ourselves. The government is no different from anyone else. They can be hung by debt. Their deficit is in the trillions of dollars, and ours is maybe $600. What happens is that we run out of money and continue to borrow until we can't borrow anymore. That is almost the situation with the world: we can't borrow anymore. What do we do now? The answer to that question brings me to the present topic called the order of things.

We must start at the present world as we know it, beginning with Noah, the last remnant of the first man, Adam, who was made in God's image and likeness. Adam was a perfect man until he became separated from God by the sin of disobedience. The world committed more and more sin from Cain's murder of his brother, Abel, to lying, cheating, and stealing, much the same as today.

The world was in such a mess that it caused God to contemplate destroying it, but Noah found favor in God's eyes and was considered righteous. And God ordered him to build an ark to save his family—his wife and his three sons and their wives, a total of eight persons—along with male and female animals of every known creation. Thus, Noah became the father of the present world.

The world evolved from the sin of Adam to more and more sin until God finally had enough and decided to destroy it. God destroyed the previous world by a flood because of the sin of Adam, the father of sin. Noah, his wife, and his three sons and their wives were left to populate the world. These eight people were as close to being without sin as possible, but they were not perfect. Only God and His Son, Jesus, are perfect. Noah and his family were tasked with replenishing the world, the same job given to Adam and Eve: be fruitful and multiply.

But guess what? Sin never did totally leave us. It continues today. Humankind's laws have almost replaced God's laws. Sin continued to progress from Adam through generations of people and continued to grieve God even after His covenant with Noah that He would not destroy the world a second time with a flood or any other major catastrophe. It so grieved God that humankind's life span was shortened to 120 years when God said, "My spirit will not contend with man forever, for he is mortal, his days will be 120 years." See Genesis 6:1–22 KJV for the entire story. Sometime later, humankind's life span was reduced to three scores and ten for a total of seventy years because of the continued iniquities of man. See Psalm 90:10 KJV for this reference and the remainder of the psalm for the reasons why God remained so displeased.

There have been many major and minor players in the order of things since Noah, but we have chosen our dear brother, Abraham, to be the next patriarch for a reference of study. God chose Abraham to be the father of His chosen people, the Jews who were to become the vehicle that would return all people back to God after having been separated from Him by sin.

Unfortunately, they were never able to fully carry out this role because of a lack of faith and disbelief. God promised them a land flowing with milk and honey, and they did not have enough faith to claim it. It started when God told Abraham that the land of Canaan would be given to his seed as an inheritance. Genesis 11:31–32 KJV states, "And Terah took Abram his son, and Lot the son of Haran his son's son, and Sarah his daughter in law, his son Abram's wife and they went forth with them from Ur of the Chaldees to go into the land of Canaan and they came unto Haran and dwelt there."

They stayed in Haran until Abraham was seventy-five years old and God told him to leave his home and family and go into a land that He would show him. Abraham did as he was told and began his journey toward the Promised Land and pitched his tent on a mountain east of Bethel. And there he built an altar and continued onward toward the south, but ended up in Egypt due to a famine in the land. In Egypt was where he lied to Pharaoh that his wife, Sarah, who was very beautiful, was his sister because he feared that Pharaoh would kill him and claim Sarah for himself.

God punished Pharaoh with various plagues until he confronted Abraham and found out that Sarah was really Abraham's wife. For bringing so much hardship on his household, Pharaoh told them to leave Egypt, and they left and returned pretty much to the area in and around the Euphrates River, where they had begun in the land of Canaan. This area was known as Mesopotamia in biblical times and is the area described as the land between the two rivers, that is, the Tigris and Euphrates Rivers. It would be known as Iraq in our present time.

Lot and Abraham had both gotten very rich with many servants and cattle and other substances, so they reasoned they needed to separate because the land could not support the two of them. Lot was given a choice and selected the plain of Jordan because it looked good and was well watered; Abraham dwelled in the land of Canaan. Genesis 13:14–18 KJV describes this land thusly,

> And the Lord said unto Abraham, after Lot was separated from him, Lift up now your eyes and look from the place where you stand northward, and Southward, and Eastward, and westward for all the land which you see to you I will give to you and your seed forever. Then Abraham removed his tent and came and dwelt in the Plain of Mamre, which is in Hebron, and built there an altar unto the Lord.

If we examine a map of these various cities first starting with Ur and then Haran, Bethel, and Hebron, we will find they are located in and around present-day Israel, the Tigris and Euphrates Rivers, Jordan, Iraq, and Iran, situated in the Middle East as we know it today—in essence, much of the land beginning from the Persian Gulf, north to the Lebanon Mountains, south to Africa, and east to Saudi Arabia, Iraq, Iran, and Jordan. And Syria is the land that God promised to Abraham and his seed, the Jews, as their inheritance in addition to all of the land across the Jordan River.

The Jews disobeyed God from the very beginning when God allowed Moses to lead them out of Egypt to claim the land, but due to their lack of faith and disbelief, they were never able to fully do so, and God allowed them to wander in the wilderness for forty years, allowing the old generation to die out before giving them an opportunity to claim the Promised Land.

Finally, when Moses led them out of Egypt and sojourned and guided them in the wilderness for forty years, provided food and water, and fought their enemies, all they had to do was believe God and claim the land that was given to Abraham and his seed, but they never did, even to this day.

As a result, God did not allow Moses to cross over Jordan with them to claim the land, and Joshua was chosen instead. God gave them very simple instructions: cross over Jordan, occupy the land, and destroy their gods, altars, images, and all indications of their worship of these gods so they could be assured that God was a jealous God and they could not have any other God before Him. In addition, He ordered them to destroy everything in the land, including men, women, and children.

God said to them, "There is no need to fear because I am delivering the inhabitants into your hands, not by your might but by mine." It was difficult for them to fathom such an awesome task, because the inhabitants were like giants to them, and they were like grasshoppers. Instead of carrying out God's instructions, they did not kill the inhabitants but intermarried and intermingled with them and began to worship their idol gods, all of which God directly opposed.

As a result, God severely punished them by allowing other nations to enslave them and constantly fight against them, even to this day. I am afraid the plight of the Jews will never be resolved until the second coming of Jesus Christ. It has been this way since the promise to Abraham and cannot be resolved by humankind's hands. Only the hands of God can eliminate the mess in the Middle East. A hundred million soldiers in Iraq, Afghanistan, Iran, or elsewhere will never resolve this crisis. This is a job for only God.

As we reflect, the Jews still have not been able to fully occupy the Promised Land of the Middle East as we know it today. They are surrounded by nations that want to wipe them off the face of the earth and are doomed to share most of their Promised Land with unfriendly neighbors. To add to the difficulties, their half-brother, Ishmael, the father of the Muslims, shares this land with them and continues to create conflict because Muslims think Ishmael was the firstborn. It is their belief that he is the heir to the promise.

The Bible, however, clearly establishes the seed of Isaac as the chosen seed, which is the seed of the Jews and not the seed of the Muslims. Genesis 20:10–21 KJV gives us the full story. Just what is the land described as the land flowing with milk and honey? The Bible describes it as the land of Canaan, and the Canaanites occupied it.

Just where is this land of Canaan in our modern world? To get a good idea, we must look at the separation of Abraham and Lot, which describes this land. See Genesis 12 and 13 KJV for the full story. This land has not been pinpointed with certainty, but most studies indicate the chosen land began at the Persian Gulf, north to the mountains of Lebanon, west to the Mediterranean Sea, south to Egypt in Africa, and east to Saudi Arabia, Iraq, Iran, Jordan, and Syria to include present-day Israel, with the key ingredient being the crossing of the Jordan River.

Why is this area so significant in the scheme of things? Could it be that oil flows in this entire area and whoever controls this area controls the oil, thereby controlling the world and the price of oil? In essence, oil establishes the world's currency because the world is totally dependent upon oil. This entire area was God's promise to the Jews and Israel, thus the reason why everyone is so adamantly opposed to Israel and wants to destroy them.

As we reflect on our dear brother, Abraham, we see his influence as the direct link to the Middle East situation as we know it today. Abraham is both the father of the Jews through his son Isaac and the Muslims through his son Ishmael, and this volatile mixture is still reaping havoc to this day. Just think about it. Abraham is the father of two of the most dominant religions in the world, Judaism and Islam, and they mix just about as much as oil and water. Will peace ever come in this area? Perhaps neve is my analogy,

How did this come into being? We must look back at God's promise to Abraham that his seed would become a great nation and all the nations of the world would be blessed through this seed. Abraham and Sarah were both old, in their eighties and nineties, and had difficulties believing that Sarah could produce a child, as they were both barren. Sarah decided to give her young, virile maid, Hagar, an Egyptian, to Abraham to make this happen. Sure enough, Hagar had a child, and his name was Ishmael. The Bible indicates that Abraham was eighty-six years old when Ishmael was born. He was indeed the firstborn but was not the chosen seed because the chosen seed was to be done through Sarah. And sure enough, about thirteen years after the birth of Ishmael, Sarah conceived and had a child, whose name was Isaac.

Sarah was ninety, and Abraham was one hundred. God told them that Isaac was the seed by which a great nation would be created and through which all nations would be blessed. Sarah became upset with Hagar and the young boy, Ishmael, because they appeared to be making fun of her child. So she convinced Abraham to get rid of Hagar and Ishmael, but Abraham was reluctant to do so because the child was the first fruits of his loins, but he decided to send them away anyhow. However, it grieved him to do so.

God heard his and Hagar's cries and told them not to worry because Ishmael would also become the father of a great nation and would be favored by God as well. Thus, Ishmael became the father of the Muslims as we know them today, the half-brother of the Jews, with Abraham being the father of both. For a clearer understanding of this entire story, read Genesis 16 and 17.

Since the Jews disobeyed God and did not drive out all the inhabitants and were forced to live with them, they began to endure unusual hardships in the new land, and their lives were in constant turmoil, so much so that they constantly cried out to God to send a deliverer to relieve them. They saw the nations in this new land with their own gods and rulers like kings and queens, and they thought they needed a king to guide and protect them as well.

Their hearts were so hardened that they never understood the magnitude of God's blessings toward them, the parting of the Red Sea, the manna in the wilderness, the water from rocks, the pillar of cloud by day, and the pillar of fire by night. None of that mattered to them, and all they did was complain and complain. In fact, they even thought they would have been better off if they had stayed in Egypt. All of this leads me to my next patriarch in the order of things, my beloved brother, David, a man after God's own heart.

The Jews continued to cry out to God each time after they were afflicted with a curse that God promised to them because of disobedience and lack of faith. In fact, God told them that they would be abundantly blessed if they obeyed God's commandments that were outlined by Moses and cursed if they disobeyed. Deuteronomy 11, 12, and 28 KJV depicts this aspect of the blessings and curses. It is evident that many of us are still living under a curse because of the Jews' disobedience, as Israel is constantly being threatened by hostile forces. Whatever happens in Israel affects the rest of the world. Today it is Iran. Yesterday it was Palestine. And tomorrow may be Russia.

They cried for a king, and God hearkened to their cries. Saul was chosen, but he made things worse until we got to David, a man after God's own heart. God chose David, no doubt, because of his humbleness. He was the least of the brothers whom the prophet Samuel had interviewed for the job. He was tending sheep for his father, Jesse, and was like an afterthought when he was presented to Samuel.

But isn't this like what God does? He chooses the least of us sometimes to become the greatest of us. David became the greatest king of all time, but he too had a weakness. He liked women and devised a method to get Bathsheba, whom he saw when he walked out on his balcony. He sent her husband to the front lines so he would be killed, and David could have her. But David was a praying man and learned the errors of his ways after the prophet Nathan told him. In fact, God forgave him and allowed him a second chance. God allowed David to almost singlehandedly destroy all of the nations in the Promised Land, but even the great David could not do so because God's chosen people's hearts were so hardened that it would take a power greater than David to redeem God's people. That power led to more and more prophets until all of them failed, and the Jews are still wandering in the wilderness to this day. So, it behooves me to say that the second coming of the final prophet, Jesus the Christ, is our and their only solution, because they killed even Him in His first coming.

Will there be total peace in our lifetime? Our only possibility is to usher in a new beginning. A new beginning is the ending of the beginning. The ending of the beginning is the beginning of Jesus, and the ending of the beginning is the death of Jesus. A new beginning is a return to the way things were when Christ ascended into heaven and told us as disciples to go out into all the world and recruit disciples for Jesus, to baptize them in the name of the Father, Son, and Holy Ghost. "And lo I am with you even to the end of the world." This should not become our job to usher in a new beginning.

Go into the hedges and highways and seek people to repent and be baptized for the remission of sins, for that is the duty of humankind. Visit our website, www.gangsforjesus.net. For our religious perspectives on subjects such as drugs, same-sex marriage, investments, and a host of more than forty modules of secular and religious writing, such as "Repent and Live or Stay Wicked and Die" or "Why Is the World in Such a Mess?" Request a free copy of your favorite module, which just so happens to be the motto of our organization, Gangs for Jesus: "Don't forget the recruits."

Our ultimate goal is to bring peace throughout the world by a serious sharing of our wealth. This subject is talked about today when more than fourteen years ago I wrote and discussed it in the introduction to our website, www.gangsforjesus.net and our Facebook page, Gangs for Jesus. If the rich man in the Bible were unable to do this, then it is almost impossible for humankind to agree to such a thing. That, however, is the goal of our organization. Be Blessed in your life endeavors.

The Riches of the Righteous

God meant for humankind to prosper or be rich, but with a stipulation: that humankind must be righteous. Righteousness and riches are a team. The odds are 100 percent that if you are righteous, riches will come with it. That was proven with Solomon when God rewarded him with riches of unimaginable size because Solomon did not seek riches from God but wisdom to be able to judge how to treat people or govern them according to the principles of God, that is, through God's mercy and grace. Mercy allows God to help us, and grace allows Him to forgive us. Without these two principles, humankind would perish because they were born to sin from the very beginning. The apostle Paul said it best, "For all have sinned and come short of the glory of God."

This is still true today, for we have all sinned and fall short of God's grace to help us. But despite all of our sins, God will help us if only we would ask Him. Asking God to help is the first step in becoming righteous. You must believe that God can do it better than we can and then step aside and let God have His way. When you are able to do this and your whole being is predicated on the principles of God, righteousness and riches will become a team, because God has promised that the righteous shall be like a tree planted by the waters that bring forth His fruit in His season. His leaves shall not wither, and whatsoever He does shall prosper. Psalm 1 talks about this, but to truly highlight what is meant about righteousness and prosperity, read Psalm 92:12–15 KJV:

> The righteousness shall flourish like the palm tree; he shall grow like a cedar in Lebanon. Those that be planted in the house of the Lord shall flourish in the courts of our Lord. They shall still bring forth fruit in old age; they shall be fat and flourishing to show that the Lord is upright; he is my rock, and there is no unrighteous in him.

God's intent for humankind is to prosper, and to do so, we must be righteous. Are any of us righteous? Perhaps none. We are still falling short. There are many of us who are rich, but are we righteous? The answer is no because riches do not lead to righteousness. But if we are righteous, riches will come. Therefore, seek righteousness instead of riches.

The Spirit God

Two totally different forces—the Spirit of God and the spirit of humankind—control the world. The question then becomes: What is the Spirit of God? What is the spirit of humankind? The answers to all questions in the universe can be found in the Bible. You just need to know where to find them. The first book of the Bible is Genesis. The answer to the Spirit of God is found in Genesis 1:1–3 KJV.

> In the beginning God created the heaven and the earth. And the earth was without form, and void; and darkness was upon the face of the deep. And the Spirit of God moved upon the face of the waters. And God said, Let there be light: and there was light.

The Spirit of God is therefore the Word of God. When God speaks, everything comes into existence. Genesis 1 concerns the creation of the world. The central theme is God saying "let there be something," and it comes into existence.

For example, God says in Genesis 1:6 KJV, "Let there be a firmament in the midst of the water and let it divide the water from the waters." At this point, God was creating heaven and earth. The firmament above was heaven, and the firmament below was earth. God said, "Let there be light in the firmament of heaven to divide day from the night." At this point, He was making day and night.

Later in the scheme of the creation, God said, "Let us make man in our image and it was done." The point I am making is that when God speaks, something must happen. That something is the Spirit of God moving upon the face of the universe to create what God chooses. The Spirit of God is therefore the world of God.

God speaks, and something that God chooses comes into existence. Humankind must accept the Word of God to be in harmony with God, or they are doomed to failure. When God breathed into Adam and Adam became a living soul, the Spirit of God was instilled into humankind through the Holy Spirit. The Holy Spirit is that inner voice that guides us as we embark on our daily activities. That inner voice tells when we are doing right or wrong or creates peace or turmoil in our lives. We become harmonious with God's plan for humankind when our lives are imbued with the Holy Spirit. To corroborate what the Spirit of God refers to, read John 1, which begins by saying,

> In the beginning was the word, and the word was with God, and the word was God. The same was in the beginning with God; all things were made by Him and without Him were not anything made that was made. And the word was made flesh and dwelt among us and we beheld His glory, the glory as of the only begotten of the father full of grace and truth. That word is Jesus Christ who was sent into the world to bear witness to His Father, the creator of everything that has been made. The spirit of God is therefore the word of God as spoken through Jesus Christ the Son of God.

It goes on to say that the law was given by Moses, but grace and truth came by Jesus Christ as the guiding force in our lives, which creates a unity of the Father, the Son, and the Holy Spirit. Isaiah 39:8 states, "The grass withers, the flowers fades but the word of God shall stand forever." When Adam was created, God gave him the Holy Spirit because He made Adam in His image, which is holy. Therefore, humankind was made holy.

The Bible says God breathed on Adam, and Adam became a living soul. At that point, humankind was endowed with the Holy Spirit, which is the Spirit of God. Then, humankind was made perfect and remained that way under the influence of the Holy Spirit until they fell from God's grace because of sin. When humankind sinned from the very first act of disobedience, they were no longer under the Spirit of God but were immediately under the spirit of humankind, which is the spirit of sin. At this point, they became separated from God due to sin and remains separated until they are redeemed through Jesus Christ, the Son of God.

Jesus is the bridge that leads humankind back to God when we accept Him as our personal Savior and are led back to God through His grace and mercy. The Spirit of God is therefore the Word of God through His Son, Jesus, who was sent into the world to bridge the gap between humankind and God by paying a ransom for our sins by dying on the cross and shedding His blood to redeem humankind from their sins. In order to receive the Spirit of God, the Holy Spirit, or the Holy Ghost all over again, we must accept Jesus as our personal Savior and repent and turn away from the spirit of humankind, the spirit of sin.

The spirit of humankind is directly the opposite of the Spirit of God. The devil governs the spirit of humankind. Revelation 12:7–12 KJV states,

> And there was a war in heaven: Michael and his angels fought against the dragon; and the dragon fought and his angels and did not win and the great dragon was cast out, the old serpent, called the Devil and Satan, which deceived the whole world was cast into the earth; and his angels were cast out with him. Therefore rejoice, you heavens, and you that dwell in them but woe to the inhabitants of the earth and of the sea for the Devil is come unto you having great wrath, because he know that he has but a short time.

The spirit of humankind came into existence when humans first disobeyed God and fell into sin. The spirit of humankind is therefore sin. Humans are born into sin and will continue in sin until they die, unless the Spirit of God returns to their lives through humankind's acceptance of Jesus Christ as their personal Savior. Nothing but the blood of Jesus can wash away my sins.

The Spirit of God cannot come into our lives unless we have faith enough to accept Jesus as Lord and personal Savior and take up our cross and follow Him. The only way that this is possible is to turn away from the spirit of humankind, which is sin, and turn to the Holy Spirit, which is the Word of God through His Son, Jesus Christ.

The only way that this can be achieved is through faith and the working of faith. Read Hebrews 11 KJV, beginning with the first verse, which states, "Faith is the substance of things hoped for the evidence of things not seen." We must rely on God's workings to do what He chooses to do with our lives instead of relying on ourselves to do something we have no control over. We must do this based on blind trust.

Unless we can do this, we will never receive the Holy Spirit or the Holy Ghost, and our lives will continue to be under the influence of humankind, which is the spirit of the devil through sin and not under the Spirit of God, which is love. "For God so loved the world that he gave his only begotten son that whosoever believes in him should not perish but should have everlasting life" (John 3:16 KJV).

Why Is the World in Such a Mess?

T he world is in a mess today because God's kingdom has become humankind's kingdom through the government and man-made laws that have watered down the kingdom of God. The rulers of the earth work against the kingdom of God. It goes all the way back to the day of the Pentecost. "All people were on one accord and all that believed were together, and all things common" (Acts 2:44) KJV). "They sold their possession and goods and parted them to all men, as every man had needs" (Acts 2:45 KJV). "And they continue to break bread from house to house and did eat with gladness and a singleness of heart."

They were on one accord, praising God and having favor with all people, and God blessed the church and added to it daily. The kingdom of God is a two-way street. You give all you have to God, and He rewards you with your heart's desires. No one would ever be in need. The church would be able to distribute to the needy as necessary. This simple analogy is what the true kingdom of God is all about. Give all that you have (your total self, not necessarily money) to God, and you will receive a multitude of blessings and riches beyond measure. The kingdom of God is like a two-way street. Give to God; receive from God. The more you give, the more you receive.

The whole theme of the Pentecost was that the church was in charge. Jesus had ascended into heaven and left specific instructions to his apostles to go out into all the world and preach the gospel to every creature.

> He that believe and is baptized shall be saved; but he that believe not shall be damned. And these signs shall follow them that believe; in my name shall they cast out devils. They shall speak with new tongues. They shall take up serpents; and if they drink any deadly thing it shall not hurt them. They shall lay hands on the sick and they shall recover.

The church, headed by the twelve apostles and later by Paul, took off like a blazing fire and nearly took over the entire world. Rome was afraid. As more and more people were converted to Christianity, more and more money flowed into the church, and the Roman government saw the writing on the wall. They would lose everything to this new Christianity and had to devise a method to destroy it. Persecution became the way to do it.

Anyone who described his- or herself as a Christian was exposed to the greatest persecution, such as beatings, prisons, and hangings, or crucifixions as the ultimate form of persecution. The more these Christians were persecuted, the stronger they became. And the recruiting became even greater. The idea was to become a martyr, just like Christ had become a martyr for humankind by dying on the cross to save a sinner like me. Stephen, James, John the Baptist, Peter, John, Paul, and many others were either killed or exiled to all kinds of disdainful places, such as the island of Patmos, where John was sent.

The church was unstoppable and threatened to become the force that the Roman government could not control. The kingdom of God had reached its apex, and Rome had to devise a method to defuse this volatile situation. Persecution was not working except to a minor degree. The Roman government was the first government to alter or modify the kingdom of God, the religion that Jesus and His disciples had taught after His ascension. Their goal was to stop the power of the church and restore power to the Roman government. They did this based on an infiltration of the church, agreeing to lessen the severity of the persecutions, getting the Christians to take a less demanding position regarding Christ as He compared to Caesar and a host of less threatening positions on religions.

Within a hundred years after Christ had ascended to heaven, the whole fiber of the church had changed. By this time, Jerusalem had fallen, human values were substituted for spiritual values, and Jesus Christ had become less and less important. The papacy had begun in its infant stages. Humankind's kingdom over God's kingdom was about to ushered in.

By the fourth century, under Constantine, Catholicism was already in place. Humankind was about to become the central figure in the church under the leadership of the pope and a bunch of symbols of the Virgin Mary and other saints. The church had been successfully converted from the Church of God to the Church of Humankind. Satan has successfully invaded the church and continues to rule until today.

Our goals as Christians are to return to the day of Pentecost and reclaim the church as the governing body instead of allowing the government to control religion. Do you realize that prayer in schools was outlawed by a Supreme Court vote of five to four and abortion was made law by the same vote of five to four? In essence, five people changed the entire course of history by a vote of five to four, a grand total of nine people. Do you realize that approximately twenty states have gay and lesbian marriages?

What a mess the world is in today. This same kind of ideology has invaded the church, and there are churches that are not speaking out strongly against it. God's kingdom has become humankind's kingdom, the kingdom of Satan.

What must we do to be saved? Peter said on the day of Pentecost, "Repent and be baptized everyone of you in the name of Jesus Christ for the remission of sins, and you shall receive the gift of the Holy Ghost." The world needs to go back to Pentecostal experience in order to save itself. The government's role today should be as the Bible states, "Be wise now therefore, O you kings, be instructed, you judges of the earth serve the Lord with fear and rejoice with trembling. Kiss the Son unless he becomes angry and you perish from the way, when his wrath is kindled but a little. Blessed are they that put their trust in the Lord."

I'm afraid the government is already headed to destruction when things like abortions, same-sex marriages, and removal of prayer from schools are passed into law to further corrupt society. Satan is in his glory. Oh, what a mess the world is in!

About the Author

T he question of "Who am I?" has confounded humankind since the beginning of time and will continue to baffle humankind until the end of time. This is one of the many questions that cannot be answered in its entirety. We can speculate, but no one truly knows.

My name is Thomas Rembert Jr. I was born in Sumter County, South Carolina, on April 5, 1944. I am the oldest of two sons born to Thomas Rembert and Susie Mae Moses. I grew up near the town of Oswego, where my father performed duties as a sharecropper until our family moved to the big city of Sumter when I was about thirteen.

As a youngster growing up in the country, I was thought of as having a brilliant mind. I was smart as hell at Clarks Elementary School, followed by Eastern High School and finally Lincoln High School, where I was selected as one of the thirteen students allowed to skip the tenth grade and begin the eleventh, allowing me to graduate in three years instead of four. We were considered the cream of the crop.

I graduated with honors in 1961, one year before my expected graduation date. I was indeed a hotshot and wanted to go to the University of South Carolina but was not permitted due to segregation. So I went to SC State College instead. This was the best move that I could have made. Not only did I get a great education in the books, but I received a great education in the sociology and psychology of life, which has helped to shape my life to this very day.

After graduating from SC State in 1966, I was drafted into the army, as the Vietnam War was in full bloom. I avoided going to Vietnam by agreeing to enlist for three years instead of the draft status of two years. I was always a man of peace and did not want to fight in a war that was in opposition to my belief of "make love, not war."

After a discharge from military duty in January 1970, I began a career with the New York City Housing Authority that would last for twenty-nine years. I was thrust deep into the ranks of the downtrodden, where welfare, poverty, drugs, and prostitution helped to shape my psyche.

Indeed, a small-town country boy had jumped out of the frying pan and dead into the fire. The projects, as they were called, were a factory of mothers making babies to get more welfare and food stamps. Very few people had jobs, so the ranks of the downtrodden continued to grow, and it became my lifelong obsession to do something about it.

As I rose through the ranks from housing assistant to assistant manager and finally housing manager, I was able to confront some of the many perils that families were facing in the projects. I held project meetings to instill a sense of pride and aspiration in my tenants and created tenant patrols to help with the growing epidemic of drugs in our buildings. I began a letter-writing campaign to social agencies and local businesses to provide summer jobs for the youths and job-training programs for the adults. I was also able to work with the housing police force and was able to set up sting operations to evict drug traffickers and halt other deviant activities, like prostitution.

Along the way I became a successful real estate broker, children's counselor, and tax preparer, which helped to thrust me into my writing career. My goal was always to help others achieve greatness through high aspiration. My writings have helped me do just that. Please follow me on my website at www.gangsforjesus.net and also on Facebook.

Printed in the United States
By Bookmasters